The Siren Call
of a Dangerous God

Essays in Evangelical Dialectic

Geoff**Ryan**

credo
PRESS

2004

Printed in Canada

National Library of Canada Cataloguing in Publication

Ryan, Geoff, 1962-
       The siren call of a dangerous god : essays in evangelical dialectic / Geoff Ryan.

ISBN 0-9735263-0-0

       1. Evangelicalism. I. Title.

BL626.3.R93 2004   230'.04624   C2004-902044-7

DEDICATED TO THE MEMORY OF

Scot "Buck" McCallum

1961 – 2003

*Orwell believed that a writer's chief responsibility
is to tell readers what they don't want to hear.*

CHRISTOPHER HITCHENS

*"Own only what you can carry with you: know languages, know
countries, know people. Let your memory be your travel bag."*

ALEXANDER SOLZHENITSYN

Contents

VI The Siren Call of a Dangerous God

.

.

Preface

I F THE ESSAY IS ANYTHING, IT IS THE DISCOURSE OF THE INEXPERT. BUT IN A society that produces ever greater numbers of experts, with an ever-increasing number of subjects in which such people claim expertise, the cultural gaps that the essayist is called upon to fill grow fewer and narrower. Still, there are a number of human concerns—mostly pertaining to what used to be called manners and morals—about which the essayist retains some plausible claim to having something valuable to say... One of the recurrent strategies of the essay is to proclaim, or gradually discover, the instability of our distinctions between the important and the trivial". (Alan Jacobs, *A Visit to Vanity Fair: Moral Essays on the Present Age*)

"Hitchens bemoans the loss of skills of dialetical thinking evident in contemporary society and the sacrifice of true irony, satire and other forms of critical style. He understands the importance of disagreement—to personal integrity, to informed discussion, to true progress..." (on Christopher Hitchen's, *Letters to a Young Contrarian*)

Imagine if you are able, a place somewhere between the scornful disbelief of the columnist Hitchens and the gracious skepticism of the college professor Jacobs. It is somewhere in that place that this collection of essays aspires to belong.

Christopher Hitchens is an atheist but his relentless quest for truth may eventually lead him to God, though likely not to the Church. He is too honest to live a lie his whole life. In the meantime, his breadth of knowledge, command of rhetoric and argument and his sheer worldliness constitute a rebuke to the ever-present shadow of anti-thought that plagues the evangelical community.

Alan Jacobs is nowhere near as fierce as Hitchens. He is quite gracious, as befits a believer—wry rather than mocking, principled more than polemical and utterly lacking in pretension. His humour, clear eye and relentless nose for truth will likely be paid more attention by those on the edges of the Church, rather than those deeper within. He is a likeable prophet, nevertheless.

The Siren Call of a Dangerous God owes much to both Hitchens and Jacobs and their respective volumes, *Letters to a Young Contrarian* and *A Visit to Vanity Fair*. I have looked to them as my two muses, a cartoon devil on one shoulder and an angel on the other, whispering and wisecracking their wisdom in my ears. I am not as clever as Hitchens, but I fear far more quixotic. Lacking the education and discipline of Jacobs, I offer up instead my varied tutelage in the university of life, as did Gorky.

My debt extends to others besides these two. Francis Bacon, Graham Greene, Laurens van der Post, Robert Kaplan, David Remnick, Tatyana Tolstaya, P.J. O'Rourke and others. None of these I have ever met or am ever to meet, but their essays and other writings have also in turn prompted and nudged me into print.

My real job is as an officer in The Salvation Army. This curious branch of the evangelical family tree is the denominational context that grounds and informs the experiences recorded in these essays. However, any application a reader cares to accept from anything read will go beyond the boundaries of one particular expression of evangelicalism. I believe this will be self-evident in the reading of these essays.

I spent the last decade of the twentieth-century living in Russia. This enchanting and tragic land has provided the material for almost half of the essays in the book. The back alleys, mean streets and housing projects of Toronto's inner city inspired the other half. My faith and religion and understanding of the world has largely been forged in these similar, though different, worlds.

"What is truth?" asked Pilate.

"Know the truth and it will set you free", promised Jesus.

A question and a promise. Good places to start.

Geoff Ryan
TORONTO, *Spring 2004*

Foreword

T HERE ARE TWO REASONS FOR MY ADMIRATION OF GEOFF Ryan: the way he lives and the way he writes. I admire Geoff for the way he lives because he has stubbornly refused to heed the call of the contemporary world to a life of comfort and contentment. Whether in the wilds of Russia, the battlegrounds of Chechnya or the mean streets of downtown Toronto, he has insisted on living and working amongst the poor and hurting, where every memory is a scar and life itself is a wound. There are easy roads in all of our lives but Geoff, and his wife Sandra, have taken none of them. Geoff applies the same, stubborn passion to the organisation that employs him, infuriates him and gives his life meaning: The Salvation Army. In some ways he is one of the most progressive thinkers in the Army; urging it forward to embrace the 21st century, while in other ways he is deeply traditional; holding unswerving to the values of daring and sacrifice by which Booth's followers were first formed. The paper on which this book is printed may be crisp and white, and the font and ink entirely up to date, but all the same, there is the unmistakable odour of Victorian reforming zeal and of the raw, heartfelt love for others that first warranted the words "Blood and Fire". As an outsider to The Salvation Army, I have found insights here that have deepened my awareness of the DNA of this historic movement and increased my admiration for both its founders and frontline heroes.

I also admire Geoff for the way he writes because he has reclaimed the 'essay': a short-form rhetoric that sits somewhere between a poem and a sermon and requires a writer who is eloquent and honest, acute in observation, insatiable in curiosity and unflinching in self-disclosure. Essay writing is one of the great traditions of North American literature, but one that has fallen into disuse in recent years. There may be many reasons for this, but one is the popular assumption that we no longer live in an idea-forming age. The essayists of the 19th and 20th century expressed, examined and explored the great ideas by which their centuries were shaped. The sickly complacency that has settled over our consumer culture in recent years has smothered such explorations, leaving only madmen, fools and fanatics to believe that ideas matter. Which of these categories Geoff Ryan belongs to I will leave the reader to decide: but he belongs without doubt to the tradition of idea-shaping essayists. You may not warm to every conclusion he draws, but you will not be left indifferent by his prose.

There is a restlessness in Geoff's writing, as if each essay were an attempt to understand something that is ultimately beyond understanding but that calls us to try nonetheless. Why does a loving creator tolerate such suffering in the world he has created? Why are even my most selfless decisions tainted by longings for comfort and safety? Why is the act of giving a cup of hot soup to a man whose life is only 'lived' in the sense that he breathes in and out and is still sentient at the end of each horrific day somehow—despite its strategic insignificance and global unimportance—the most meaningful act in which I can engage? Geoff does not attempt to answer these questions, but to do something far more important—to ask them. His message is that it is when we stop asking these questions that we cease to be human and that though you may spend a lifetime wrestling and never reach an answer, you will have lived a better life for asking. "Each of us visits this earth involuntarily, and without an invitation", Albert Einstein wrote, "For me, it is enough to wonder at the secrets".

I have been stirred and challenged by these essays. More than once I have been forced to re-examine the roots and reasons of my own comfortable, post-modern faith. Have I, along with my culture, opted for what a close friend recently called 'a padded cross'? In my sincere desire to be relevant, in my terrible fear of being labelled a fanatic, have I sold out the faith I profess? It is not our DVD players and mobile phones that make us human, it is love. This book is a reminder that there is a love that has touched our world in the past and that can touch it again. The seeds of our humanity are not lost forever, just buried deep in the frozen soil of our consumer winter. May these essays play their part in thawing us.

Gerard Kelly
Co-Director, The Bless Network
The Midlands, England

Chapter 1: Not to Reason Why

"If knowing answers to life's questions is absolutely necessary to you, then forget the journey. You will never make it, for this is a journey of unknowables —of unanswered questions, enigmas, incomprehensibles, and most of all, things unfair."
—Madame Jean Guyon

"The question of why evil exists is not a theological question, for it assumes that it is possible to go behind the existence forced upon us as sinners. If we could answer it then we would not be sinners. We could make something else responsible. Therefore the "question of why" can always only be answered with the "that" which burdens man completely."
—Dietrich Bonhoeffer, *Creation and Fall/Temptation*

* Names have been changed

ATIMA WAS THREE YEARS OLD—A YEAR OLDER THAN MY daughter, a year younger than my youngest son. She had two days to live. She lay in the middle of a hospital bed, arms and legs straight like a stick figure, wrapped in blood-stained gauze to cover the burns on 70% of her body. Her face was burned too. Tubes snaked out of her nostrils. The only movement, the only sign of life, came from her eyes. They were wide open and followed me as I moved around the room, large and brown and wet. Her breath came in short gasps as drawn out breaths caused too much pain.

Fatima was a Chechen and she died in that hospital bed in the city of Nazran in the Muslim Republic of Ingushetia, Southern Russia. The Second Chechen War, as it is becoming known, is a brutal conflict with a history behind it stretching back several hundred years. It is a particularly nasty example of the religio-ethnic, semi-nationalistic 'peoples war' that have characterized the declining years of the 20th century. 'There is no one to root for in this mess of a war' wrote Colin McMahon of the *Chicago Tribune*. He is dead right.

Fatima was in the kitchen of her house in a small village in the Chechen interior when a flying piece of shrapnel from a rocket exploded into the hot water tank spewing boiling water all over her. At the border crossing into Ingushetia, the soldiers would not let her mother cross with her for three days. During those days, winter days, she lay in the open air, on the side of the road, with her open burns. By the time they were permitted to cross and made it to the hospital in Nazran, it was far too late.

As the nurses changed the bandages for the last time on the day she died, silent tears flowed out of Fatima's eyes to stain her pillow. She never complained and died with her eyes open, they simply stopped blinking, stopped watching, stopped seeing. One final, painful breath.

I fled the hospital that day and stood outside gulping in the fresh air on the street. I breathed in huge drawn-out breaths to compensate for what Fatima wanted to do, but could not. My project manager for the relief effort we are running in Ingushetia and Chechnya, was quiet and tense. He is a Chechen, a Muslim, a refugee like Fatima. 'I have a daughter her age', he stated. I knew his story and knew that he has, in fact, five daughters. At the beginning of our acquaintance I foolishly asked, 'no sons?', knowing how important sons are in the patriarchal Chechen culture. 'I had two sons', he replied stonily. 'Twins, both $1\frac{1}{2}$ years old. During the first war (1994-1996) they were hiding in our basement with their grandmother during an attack. A trooper threw a grenade into the basement.'

I can still see Fatima's small face at night sometimes. Bright child eyes—much like my daughter's. I can hear the short, sharp struggling gasps of air. I can smell the presence of death in the hospital room. I can see her mother slumped in the corner of the room, unblinking with Islamic resignation: 'If Allah wills...'. I think of the soldiers in the planes who bombed the village and the ones at the checkpoint who rejected the small amount of money that Fatima's mother offered them as a bribe. How much is the life of a three-year old worth? Does the price go up in a war zone? I imagine what I would do to them if I could get my hands on them.

In spite of my theological training, in spite of myself, I could easily wonder where God was. I do not allow myself to. I never said a word further to my manager about this. We were silent together. He as a fatalistic Muslim. Me—a realist who has made a deal with God.

* * *

I am over 40 years old now. I have lived in three different countries, traveled in over 25 and seen something of life. For nine years I lived in Russia, serving as an officer in The Salvation Army.

Since my arrival in that land a month before the coup that ended Communism in 1991, I have changed much and learnt much. As one writer has noted, Russia marks people. Some it makes exquisite, others it cripples.

I like to think of myself as a realist and as such, have come to a firm realization, a firm conviction, on three matters. I have 'worked them out' over the years of my life to date, in a hundred engagements with the enemy, with much 'fear and trembling' as required by the Scriptures.

The first conviction is this: Not every problem has a solution. The second one is: Life is not fair. The third one is with regard to the existence of evil in the world: The question is not to ask 'why?', but rather—'what now?' There is no point on speculating why it exists and why God allows it. Far better to acknowledge the facts before one and deal with these.

These are more than convictions of mine, to me they are proven facts—slow in coming but steadily forged over years as a soldier in the fight of faith. They cannot be disproved to me. They form a paradigm that allows me to fight the battles God has sent me into. They allow me to survive, to get through the night. Bear with me as I continue the retelling of three encounters of recent months by way of explanation.

* * *

'I'm afraid to say it... to say what I am really thinking.'
It was quiet and warm in the car and snow was falling outside. Tears formed in the corners of her large eyes as she bowed her head and stared unseeing into her lap.

I had known Natasha for over a decade at that point, starting from the time she wandered into one of our first meetings in the city then known as Leningrad, now called St. Petersburg. It was early autumn 1991. She was saved, joined our church, started working in ministry fulltime. She was eighteen then. Born and raised in Kazakhstan in

Central Asia, at seventeen Natasha left home to become an actress. She did not make the stage, instead she found us. In 1994, Natasha moved south to Rostov-on-Don as part of a team assisting my wife and myself as we church planted in that region.

Three days after arriving in Rostov, Natasha received a call from home—her Father had died of alcohol poisoning. She went back home to Alma- Ata to bury him and then returned to us. The other team members went back north after a year while Natasha stayed.

I have never met anyone with a gift for working with children like Natasha. She can work magic with them, becoming one with their world yet remaining apart, moving easily in and out and never really belonging in either. Now over 30, she remains the most perplexing combination of childish innocence and worldly guile, exuding a touching simplicity yet at times comes out with the most profound thoughts. She needs people, an audience—yet is almost painfully shy. She remains alone in the biggest crowd and her dazzling smile is marred only by the sadness in her eyes. She is an enigma. She is also now an orphan

One autumn evening the rest of her family died—her elderly mother, her older brother and his wife. Wiped out in one afternoon by a man as yet free. If Americans choose to kill mainly with guns—Russians use knives, and Natasha's family died a Russian death with no clear motive, blood splattered walls and lingering agony in the ill-equipped emergency ward of the local hospital.

At the time of our conversation, Natasha had just returned from burying the rest of her family.

'I think I hate God', she continued. I had noticed that during meetings she did not sing anymore and that her eyes remain open and staring during prayer.

'I can't sing, I can't pray, I can't even think of God without...'

The inevitable 'why' remained unspoken, but everywhere present.

She had a point. Since consecrating her life to God almost a decade before she had served faithfully, doing what we asked of her, going where we wanted—a gypsy life with no real fixed abode in often difficult places, working long hours, minimal pay. 'No personal life whatsoever' was one of her habitual sayings, said only half-jokingly. '...what does the Lord require of you? To act justly and to love mercy and to walk humbly with your God.' What more? Why then?

Her mother would visit from time to time—a simple soul, a nice lady, benign. Not asking much from life and never having received much. She believed in God, as all women her age in Russia seem to nowadays. She smiled much, like her daughter. I remember her singing a folk song one night during a campfire at one of our summer camps. 'My mother was believer', Natasha whispered, 'but my brother...' The tears came again.

Very briefly I considered defending God by explaining the complicated relationship between free will, the sovereignty of God and the terrible implications of God's refusal to win by coercion and thus the sin within and the evil around. My heart was not in it. It would not have helped.

I wanted to hold her close, comfort her and tell her that I would look after her and that nothing bad would ever happen again. This would have been a lie, though, and was not appropriate in any case. So I bought her an ice cream, assured her that the culprit would receive his punishment (if not here, then in the hereafter). 'Nothing will change what has happened', I said, 'the issue now is not why, but what next?'

I offered my help in a practical manner with the legal details. We talked no further about God.

* * *

Olga is not the type to 'rage, rage against the dying of the light', though I would if I were her. She is placid by nature, docile some would say, certainly calm and quiet. Maybe things like this happen to people like her because of this, because she lets them happen. Who can tell?

She is in her late-twenties now and came to us after having made contact with our HIV/AIDs, Drug & Alcohol Rehab Program. She came for counseling. She was eighteen at the time. Her live-in boyfriend was an addict and infected her in bed. Olga became HIV positive. The counseling helped and she started attending church.

She was saved, became a member of our church, left her job selling in the local market, took discipleship training with another Christian agency in the city then entered our own mission training program. She changed from an emotional flatliner to a smiling, cheerful follower of Jesus. 'I can't believe how I lived before,' she said, 'I feel like it was all only a dream and only now have I woken up to life!'

One night Olga's old boyfriend came calling, one thing led to another—he raped her. She became pregnant. Her grandmother insisted she get an abortion—she refused as a Christian. We suggested she put the child up for adoption—she refused as a mother. The church council allowed her to remain as a member in good standing. She had done nothing wrong, nothing at all.

The boyfriend started attending Sunday services, his motives unclear. I would shake his hand resentfully, not wanting to meet his gaze lest he read in my eyes what I truly thought of him. How could he? How could God let him ruin it all—everything was going great? Olga finally, for the first time in her short twenty years had the chance at life. She had taken hold of hope and was fashioning a future. All now ripped out and stamped out like a cigarette butt in a ten-minute scuffle in a dingy apartment on an autumn evening. The dream turned into a nightmare.

Olga stopped smiling. The baby was born. How long will she live? Will her child be HIV positive? Where does the boyfriend fit in? Olga does not ask these questions, she is too placid, too resigned. She simply does not smile anymore.

I could rage for her, it is in me—this is beyond unfair, a no-win situation for everyone, no answers in sight. But I do not rage. I shake my head and move on. I am a soldier, I know there is little point in lingering over a casualty. The medics have been called. There is nothing more for me to do here.

* * *

As a Westerner and therefore a child of the enlightenment, I am a product of rationalism. As a Protestant I am therefore uncomfortable with mystery. Every question has an answer, every problem a solution, there is always a way to figure things out and satisfy the need to know. We were given this understanding with our mother's milk.

But nine years in Russia, close engagement with the Eastern Orthodox tradition and with a nation whose thinking patterns are more Eastern than Western and who are therefore comfortable with mystery—all this has has an effect. I have changed, I think differently now.

Somewhere along the journey I stopped trying to figure out how evil came into the world; why God allows little children to suffer; why life is so unfair to some and so generous to others. I stopped asking why? To wonder why is a luxury it turns out, one that I indulged in when I had the time and space, when I could turn the problem over at arm's length, rationally and objectively weigh all sides of the issue, when it was mainly only theory that I had experienced. Then I wondered 'why?' and I wondered much about it. That was a long time ago.

Theory gave way to experience, to reality, and I found things different on the battlefield, with the enemy pressing hard and the ground slick with blood; when you are bone-tired with the fear that has been throbbing through your veins so fast for so long that it seems you will split open; when the stench of sin and evil and pain clogs your nostril and invades your lungs. When this happens, you could care less 'why' this is all happening. You are in the middle of the 'what now?' and there is no other reality. To think otherwise would be fatal, the enemy waits for such an opening. So you follow orders, parry and thrust and slash and leave the philosophers to contemplate 'why?'

And so I compromised and made a deal with God. I would no longer ask 'why?' I would live with mystery and paradox and a hundred unanswered questions and unsolvable problems. I would forget my upbringing and my heritage and learn my lessons from the long-suffering Slavs among whom God has sent me to live and work. I would put aside my ruminations and work with the 'what now?' I would fight evil and unrighteousness with all my might and save as much of the world as I could. I would focus and not allow any distractions, any luxuries, I would no longer ask 'why?'

"Theirs is not to reason why, there's but to do and die", wrote Tennyson . And I have died a hundred deaths since I made that deal—in hospital rooms, bedsides, darkened cars, back alleys and amid the carnage of war. But I have not gone back on my deal. I have fought and will continue to fight, to the very end.

When all is finished for me, however, when I have fought the good fight to the end and I stand before the Lord, bloody and scarred no doubt, but hopefully unbowed. Then I will ask of God to keep His end of the bargain.

I will talk about Natasha and Fatima and Olga and the hundreds and hundreds of others—and I will want some answers.

I will ask 'why?' I will scream it out until it fills the heavens and shakes the earth. I will deafen the angels with my 'WHY?'

Where was I when He laid the earth's foundations?

Where was He when Fatima was shivering on the ground as the infection spread through her body?

I really do not think that it will come to this, however. God is good, He keeps His promises. After all, we made a deal.

NOTE: Olga's baby was eventually diagnosed as HIV positive.

Give fire that makes men heroes, turns weakness into might,
The fire that gives the courage to suffer for the fight,
The fire that changes fearing to pentecostal daring,
The fire that makes me willing for Christ to live or die...
The world for God! The world for God!
I give my heart! I will do my part!
– Evangeline Booth

A LATE VICTORIAN HYMN WITH NEW LIFE BREATHED INTO IT BY a fiery melody fashioned by a young British musician. I sang it with conviction and abandon and fervor along with several hundred others at a missions conference for young people. We sang it very well with enthusiasm and gusto, with eyes closed and faces upturned beseeching—demanding even—satisfaction of our God, some with raised fists and many, many with tears.

But did we mean it? As a friend of mine pointed out to me—Christians do not usually tell lies, but we often sing them.

Were we lying or just it just another terminal case of youthful euphoria, the strength of our convictions being no match for the strength of our emotions? Was our singing not ragged around the edges with a whiff of fear? What if we actually had to become heroes, live lives of pentecostal daring, make the choice between living or dying? What if our hearts were asked of us, our lives?

* * *

A few months prior to that conference I had attended the funeral of a young girl in Russia. Her name was Nastia and she was eighteen years old. She was very pretty, a "girl-next-door type" with curly blond hair and a lop-sided grin. The type of girl that a guy would notice. Further, she was genuinely nice. She didn't use her looks as a weapon, to tease the boys or threaten other girls. She enhanced any company she was with.

On a hot summer Saturday night, while out for a stroll, she was hammered into unconsciousness and raped and her throat was slit. She was thrown into the nearby river Don, like an old candy wrapper—used, crumpled up and tossed away.

In Russia death comes very hard; it is unforgiving and occurs with a disheartening frequency. My wife and I buried far too many people during our time there—too many young people. There are no funeral parlors and no funeral directors. Nothing is done to deny the reality of the event, to pretty it up, to distance it from ourselves as is the case in the West. Death in Russia is up close and in your face. It mutters away in the backgound of daily life like a low constant hum, ominous elevator music, never going away, never turning off and frequently rising in volume to ear-splitting crescendos—this is what it means to be young in Russia. And in the south of Russia it gets very hot in the summer and so you bury your dead quickly because there is no embalming and the body rots.

Nastia's mother shed no tears, her face was like a stone. In her youth I imagine she had been attractive like her daughter, but Russian village life had etched itself into her face and polished her beauty into a weary hardness. I felt that she saw no one and heard nothing that day. Nastia's twelve-year-old sister did not seem aware of what was going on. She clung fiercely to Ira, Nastia's best friend, never letting her go and it was hard to tell who was comforting whom. And there was the old grandfather who just rocked back and forth and in his grief muttered curses and imprecations against fascists and Nazis. I suppose the grief mixed it all up in his mind and to his thinking the two events matched each other in awfulness. The stormtroopers coming through in 1942 was the last time something so terrible had happened to him and his family.

I paid my respects to Nastia as she lay in the open coffin under a dazzling summer sky. Her mother had tried to cover her face with what looked like a linen table cloth, but it was cheap lace and you could see through it. They had painted her up with lipstick and cosmetics, but they could not close her mouth. It remained open in a silent scream.

We walked through the dusty village streets to the graveyard. In Russian burials, the coffin is nailed shut, lowered into the ground and then everyone takes three handfuls of dirt to throw on the coffin, an Orthodox tradition with some obscure link to the Trinity and a vague superstition about the resurrection. So with everyone else, I took my handful of dirt, and threw it on the coffin of Nastia as the ground swallowed her up.

After the funeral, I drove back home and walked into our yard. I wanted, needed, to see my daughter Anya, who was one-year old at the time. When I had found out that my wife was expecting again I feared having a girl, I must confess. We already had two boys and another one would have been fine with me. I was afraid of the vulnerability that a girl would bring into our home and into my life. In Nastia's death and funeral my worst fears had been realised. I found

Anya sitting in a chair, an older lady from our church was looking after her. As I bent over her all I could see was Nastia lying there with her mouth open. I wanted to touch Anya and stroke her face, but as I did the dirt from Nastia's grave loosened from under my fingernails and left a faint muddy trace on her left cheek. 'My God, what sort of a world have I brought you into?', I said to myself, to my daughter and to no-one in particular.

Two days later I stood in front of several hundred young people at a regional youth event. Nastia should have been there. As I looked at them I felt moved to ask that question again, 'What sort of world do we live in? What sort of world have we brought you in to? What sort of world have we left you?'

* * *

It is an extreme world, in which there are usually over thirty wars raging at any given time with people killing each other even as you read this. It is a world in which in the space of time it takes us to complete an average evangelical worship service, eight thousand people will have starved to death or died of hunger- related diseases. Two thousand of those will have been children. It is a world in which all too often 18-year-old girls do not get to grow up and do not get to attend youth events. That is the world my daughter is growing up in, if she makes it past Nastia's age. That is the 21st century and that is your inheritance if you are young. That is the reality.

However, as a Christian I cling to a different vision, a different reality—I believe it is out there, I know it is. The Bible gives fragments of this new, different, better world; a quick glimpse like a burst of sunlight flashing off the crest of a wave, like a few bars of music snatched by the evening breeze and tantalizingly carried past our ears—hints, reminders, clues, promises.

Psalm 144 is such a vision—a painting of a different world and a different millennium. It presents a vision worth living and dying for and tells me how to get there. It constitutes to me the ultimate challenge for the restless energy and yearning idealism of youth. A battle hymn as song of praise as prayer. An "I dare you", from God.

"Then our sons in their youth will be like well-nurtured plants, and our daughters will be like pillars carved to adorn a palace. Our barns will be filled with every kind of provision. Our sheep will increase by thousands, by tens of thousands in our fields; our oxen will draw heavy loads. There will be no breaching of walls, no going into captivity, no cry of distress in our streets. Blessed are the people of whom this is true; blessed are the people whose God is the Lord." (verses 12-15)

What a beautiful picture of a world in which our sons and daughters will grow up and grow old. Not like in Russia where young men must go into the military to come back all too often dead, maimed or with their minds destroyed; where they will not have to choose between finishing an education that will open no opportunities to earn a living or joining the 'Mafia' for a flashy, albeit short, life? It is a world where our daughters will grow up into beautiful womanhood and not end up like Nastia. It is a world where our barns will be filled and there will be food so that people in some parts of the world will not starve to death while people in other parts of the world are singing praises to God. It is a world in which pensioners will not go eight months without receiving their pension and exist on crusts of bread and the handouts of strangers. Instead, the barns will be full! There will be no breaching of walls and no captivity, there will be stability and safety; no crime, no wars ... no cry of distress in our streets! 'No cry of distress in our streets!' This is the Christian vision. This is the world that we long and work for!

This is the vision... yet the reality, for many, many people in the world, is Nastia's funeral.

So what do we do with this present reality? We have to deal with it, we know, in our heart of hearts, that it exists. What about the vision we sing about, we preach about, we pray for and dream about? The reality keeps me awake at night but the vision gets me up in the morning. How do we reconcile these two polarities? How do you get from the reality to the vision? How do you transform the reality into the vision? Are we fighting a hopeless cause?

The answer is in David's opening lines: 'Praise be to the Lord my Rock, who trains my hands for war, my fingers for battle'.

How do we change our reality into God's vision? The reality will not change on its own and the vision will not suddenly be born out of nothingness. It will not happen without a fight, it has to be taken by force, forged in battle. There is a powerful scene in the film *First Knight*. The evil Mordred has burst in upon King Arthur and his knights seated at the round table, the heart of his kingdom of Camelot. Mordred is making demands and uttering threats that Arthur will not concede to. So he is threatened with war—a war that will destroy the peace and tranquility of his life and his kingdom. Arthur fixes Mordred with a steady eye and tells him that if it is war he wants then war he will get because sometimes, 'There is a peace to be found only on the other side of war.'

There is a spiritual war raging for the souls of men and women; there is a war for a broken, dying world out of which God will make a rightly ordered society. Yes, there is a battle raging and there is a call to commit to the war, to fight for the vision, to fight for a different better reality and the prize is hope.

But wars are fought by people, by soldiers. What sort of soldiers? Who is needed? 'Down these mean streets must come a man who himself is not mean, neither is he tarnished nor afraid', wrote the novelist Raymond Chandler. Down the mean streets and alleyways of the world there lives an expectation, a longing, a deep need for men and women who not only do good, but who are good themselves. People untarnished, holy and above the dirt and the filth and the pain through which they walk. People most of all, who are not afraid.

We talk a lot about this in the church. We know the gospel imperative to mission. We accept the need to be cleansed, the need for holiness, the need to be above the sin that surrounds us. The need to be a clean, pure and holy people.

But that is not the hard part, is it? The hard part is the fear.

We can admit to unholiness and face up to it. That is what Sunday morning services are for with its altar calls. That is what youth events and conferences are for. We have ways of dealing with this. But the fear, what to do with the fear?

Many of us are fearful—afraid to give up things, give up people, give up plans and dreams, afraid to go places, afraid to really live an extreme life for Jesus.

We talk of being radical but extend it no further than skateboards and clothing fashions. We talk of life on the edge but live in a comfort zone so far from any edge that the fear of falling over that edge is ludicrously remote. The surrounding culture (both inside and outside the church), its values and priorities, steadily erode our risk potential as our parents and peers urge us to get the best deal out of life. We gradually conform ourselves to everyones else's expectations and fears. We exchange the chance to have a life in order to simply make a living. We make peace with fear and content ourselves with what we have been told is to be our life. The world for God? Too big a task, too much a mess, too scary a thought.

To fear is to be human and to fear is not sin—but to allow the fear to control us, make our decisions for us, run our lives...that is our sin. Love casts out all fear but we do not love enough. God so loved the world, that he gave his son. We love less, a lot less. Our parents will not give their sons or daughters, we will not give ourselves. We are indeed a sinful and unbelieving generation.

* * *

When I think about my Anya I am afraid. When I think about Nastia my fear turns into anger. Hopefully it is a holy anger. When I think about the women weeping, the men going in and out of prison, the girl on the streets, the hungry children, the millions of souls without the light of God, I—like William Booth, the founder of The Salvation Army —get angry. Angry enough to vow to fight, angry enough to declare war—in order to find to create the peace that I want for my daughter and that I hope Nastia has found. I pray that I will master my fear.

I read a powerful story about a reporter who was interviewing the commander of a teenage suicide brigade in Palestine. The newscast showed ranks of young teenagers with explosives strapped to their bodies carrying guns and marching up and down, calling on Allah and ready to die for a country they had never seen and likely never would see. The reporter was nonplussed and asked the brigade commander, "Why do they do it? Why do these young people do it? Why are they willing to go and die for a place they have never been, a place they will never get to? The young leader replied: 'Lady, none of us have ever been to Palestine, but when the west wind blows we smell it in the air and for that we will live and die.'

What are you willing to live for—really live? What are you willing to die for?

* * *

I was once in the south of Chechnya in an area where the fighting is still fairly intense. We were entering a town that no other aid agencies had made it to yet. The week before, the Chechen fighters had commenced a campaign of suicide attacks, driving trucks loaded with explosives into the Russian military checkpoints that control the roads. The Russians were tense and jumpy and we should have been more careful.

Our three vehicles drove up fast to the checkpoint outside of the town. We gave the soldiers no warning of who we were or that we were coming. One fired his machine-gun into the air in warning, yelling at us to get back. As we got out of our vehicles to explain things, he started yelling louder, at the same time backing up very fast and lowering his gun to take aim at our cars. The shots sounded like firecrackers.

With some fast talking and a lot of grace we were able to sort things out and eventually drove off unscathed. Maybe he was simply trying to scare us, maybe he was just a bad shot—I'll never know, I suppose.

It wasn't until later that night after we had made it safely back over the border to our field office in the neighbouring republic that it hit me. As the sun set over the Caucauses I sat in our guarded compound and pondered what had happened. As it was happening I was not particularly frightened—more than anything I was fascinated and a little incredulous that someone was actually shooting at me. Now in the cool of the evening, I felt the fear gnawing at my stomach.

How close did it actually come—again something that I'll never know. Still, it was a close call, a very close call and it could have turned out very differently. This much I knew for sure.

If I had died bringing help to children not much different than my own, would it have been worth it? Would my life have counted, my ministry—had I made it count? Had I stayed the course and walked my streets and alleyways in compassion, untarnished and without fear? Had my hands, trained for war, done adequate service for the King, done my part to win the world for God and create the Psalmist's vision?

Strangely enough at this moment some words came back to me that had been penned by my father as a young man and shared with me years earlier during my troubled teen years: 'It is not growing old that I fear, or even dying, it is being young and having done nothing.'

What are you willing to die for? Better yet, what are you willing to live for?

Chapter 3: The Mute Evangelist

"Commercials, catch words, political slogans, and high-flying intellectual rumors clutter our mental and spiritual space. Our minds and bodies pick them up like a dark suit picks up lint. They decorate us. We willingly emblazon messages on our shirts, caps—even the seat of our pants... We are immersed in birth-to-death and wall-to-wall "noise"—silent and not so silent."
—Dallas Willard, *The Divine Conspiracy*

"Preach at all times and if necessary, use words." —Francis of Assisi

S AYID IS A BIG MAN, HUGE IN FACT, WITH A CHEST MADE FOR stopping bullets and essentially, that is what he does for a living. He is a former policeman in the tactical squad of the major crimes division of the Ministry of Interior Affairs for the city of Grozny, the Republic of Chechnya. He still holds the rank of major in the police, has a law degree, and for a year served on the presidential guard of Aslan Maskhadov, the elected President of Chechnya and presently commander of rebel guerilla forces warring with Russia. Sayid is also a refugee and worked for The Salvation Army in our relief effort in Ingushetia and Chechnya. He was head of security for our relief operation and took care of all legal issues, liason with local police and served as the bodyguard whenever foreigners came to visit and view our operation. He is as tough as he looks, though he speaks softly and is a devout Muslim, who does not smoke or drink. He prays frequently.

Sayid lost a daughter during the first Chechen War in the mid 1990's. She died one night in his arms of an undiagnosed illness. They could not have made it to the hospital past the checkpoints as it was after curfew and the soldiers would have shot them on sight. 'When something like that happens to you, you have one of two choices', he told me, 'you can either go out and blow them all up, or you can do something to make the situation better.' He made his choice and worked with us to make things better, accepting the help we give his people, but not the faith behind it.

To a man like Sayid, talk is cheap—he has seen too much, heard too much, done too much. It is hard to impress him and earn his respect if you are a man. Even harder, if not impossible, if you are woman. In Sayid's worldview women have very specific roles and do not count much in the overall picture. He speaks of the Chechen guerillas with loathing and of the Russians with contempt. He is deferential to foreigners, but distanced.

My wife was on a visit to the aid project, accompanying a representative from our head office. I was sick and could not go. It was my wife's first time in the area. Sayid accompanied her everywhere as bodyguard, not allowing her even to go to the bathroom without accompanying her and standing outside the door. My wife is naturally friendly and talkative and so in spite of himself, Sayid found himself opening up a bit and talking about about various things with her during the course of the three days they were together, including numerous discussions about faith.

One evening Sayid invited her to his home for dinner and to

meet his wife and three children. Home was a single room rented from a local Ingush family. Sayid's apartment in the Chechen capital, Grozny, had been reduced to a pile of rubble in a Russian bombardment. On the way back to the hotel later that night Sayid asked my wife why I (as a man and as a husband) would allow her (as a woman, as my wife, as the mother to my children) to come to such a dangerous area. Implicit in the question was a puzzled disapproval. Sandra replied with a question:

'Why are you here?'

'That's different', Sayid continued, 'these are my people'.

'These are my people too', replied Sandra.

'What about your children?' he continued.

'Why are my children any more precious than your children?'

'But I don't have a choice—and you do.'

'That's why we have a lot of the problems we do in the world, the people with choices choose not to help those who have no choices.'

'We believe that if you die fighting for a good cause, you go straight to paradise—and you?'

'I believe that as a Christian we don't have to be afraid of death and that we should never let fear of death make our decisions for us.'

'You really believe that?" Sayid asked, a new respect in his voice.

'So faith without deeds is dead'.

Words without deeds, too.

* * *

In his book, *Fat Bodies, Thin Minds,* Os Guiness offers an incisive critique of the evangelical propensity toward anti-intellectualism. In one intriguing section he discusses the interplay between word and image in the Scriptures. He reminds us that the world was created by the spoken word, and that it will eventually finish in a word of judgement. To the Jews, words were a creative force, when they passed a person's lips, something was new and permanent was birthed.

In the Old Testament, seeing almost inevitably led to idolatry and therefore image and symbol were strictly controlled by God. The third commandment reveals God's concern over this issue. No person was permitted to look on the face of God and live. God communicated with his people through the Word issued out of flashing clouds and flaming bushes, in dreams and even through muttering mules. On stone tablets. The Word—spoken and written,

With the advent of Christ the Word became flesh and moved even closer to us. Paul the lawyer, trained in the art of words, laid the foundation for the Church as people of the Word. It was a world where the dominant cultures of Greece and Rome were both powered by oratory (the classical education of the Greeks was a three-stage development comprised of grammar, logic and rhetoric). The Protestant Reformation reaffirmed our allegiance as people of the Word renewing Christ's church with the rallying cry: Sola Scriptura!

But what do we do in a culture, a world, where not only the Word—but words—no longer mean what they used to? Where words have been devalued to the point of being empty vessels conveying nothing. As an Orthodox Priest from the Eastern Bloc once remarked: 'How do you communicate spirituality when words have lost their meaning?' If 'post-modernism' means anything at all then it means this.

Could it be that in virtually emptying words of meaning we become the generation that commits the ultimate blasphemy? Too many words through increased mass-media via email and the internet, TV and MTV combined with an aggressive subjectivity have birthed a world where people are either so sick of words that they will not listen or so mistrustful that they won't believe, even if they bother to listen.

In an age when truth is considered to be relative and subjective opinion has all but replaced absolute faith, words—written and spoken—lose their descriptive and prescriptive power and can end up meaning anything at all. And when something can mean anything, it ultimately means nothing. 'If you stand for nothing, you will fall for anything', observed G.K. Chesterton.

I remember watching our teenage foster daughter as she watched a music video on TV. The group performing on the video was British and the singing was in English. She is Russian and does not speak or understand English. She sat and watched the same video over and over again. Figuring I could help out by translating, I asked her if she wanted to know what they were singing about? 'It doesn't matter', she replied. 'The words don't make any difference', she said as she continued to stare at the flickering images dancing across the TV screen. It was, I believe, the voice of her generation.

What is a society like where words mean whatever the speaker wants them to mean? It is a society where, in the end, words lose all meaningful meaning and are replaced by the visual, the image, the logo. In short, it looks much like our society. The sports giant Nike made corporate history in the late 1990s by a policy decision to remove the actual word 'Nike' from all labeling, to remove all words, in fact. From now on they would only display the famous 'swoosh' in all its marketing strategy. Words were no longer needed—the symbol is enough, it says it all—or all that needs to be said.

The problem, however, is that we still tend to equate evangelism in our collective consciousness with talking, with words—the 4-spiritual laws, giving our testimony, the sinner's prayer, the crusade and altar call. Words remain our main evangelistic strategy. The dominant evangelical image at the beginning of the 21st century is a preacher or worship leader with a microphone—the preacher, the conference speaker, the singer. But we live in a culture that is flooded with words, saturated with information and facts and story to a degree where words seem to have lost all their ability to move people, to generate trust and be believed. People just do not believe what you tell them anymore.

What to do? It seems to me that one of the most important things that the present generation can do to serve the cause of Christ, is to give meaning back to words—as an act of worship, as a strategy for effective evangelism. To lend credibility to words so they mean what they are supposed to mean, so they mean something, so they once again become adequate vessels to convey ideas and truth.

The Gospels note that the main difference between Jesus and the Pharisees and Teachers of the Law was that when they spoke, Jesus' words had authority and weight and a credibility to them—a credibility lent by who he was and what he did. The lives of the Pharisees emptied anything they had to say of true meaning and worth. They were seen as hypocrites whose utterances were skeptically viewed by the common folk as religious posturing.

A good example of this occured shortly before Jesus arrest

and subsequent crucifixion—his triumphal entry into Jerusalem. What was the first thing he did, knowing that his time was limited and that the next hours would be his last opportunity to say what needed to be said, to equip his disciples, to get the message across? He cleared the Temple in an act of social justice. I believe that by this dramatic act Jesus, for the last time, invested his subsequent and final teaching with credibility and meaning, as he had throughout his three years of ministry by healing and performing miracles. As a result, the people were 'amazed at his teaching' (Mark 11:18) and 'hung on his words' (Luke 19:48).

How does this relate to evangelicals in their historical mission to be bearers of the good news? I believe it means that proclamation evangelism cannot be the only strategy. In the end it does have to come down to words, but words well chosen and backed by the weight of the speaker's life and actions. They cannot be the opening gambit or the main play, they are for clinching the deal. Actions do speak louder than words—now more than ever.

'But this is my strategy anyway', many Christians might protest. 'I rarely preach at my friends and work mates, mine is a silent witness.' Too silent, it seems. I have read a number of studies done on evangelicals in recent years, each of which concludes that basically there is little discernible difference in lifestyle between believers and nonbelievers. In lifestyle choices, core values, ethical issues, even charitable giving, the two groups are virtually indistinguishable from each other. According to statistics from the United States, well over a quarter of the population claimed to be 'born-again', but as has been pointedly asked, should not a quarter pound of salt be having more effect on a pound of meat?

Chapter 4:

The Siren Call of a Dangerous God

Sadly impractical, never conforming,
Never your spirit to prudence would bend;
Love's sweet fanatic, untiringly storming
Ramparts impregnable, young to the end.
(From the poem *To George Scott Railton* by David Guy)

ORE THAN ANYTHING ELSE, PROPHETS ARE GAMBLERS. They risk all on the chance that it really is God who is speaking to them and through them. A priest is someone different altogether. Priests hear God as scheduled in the Temple on the Sabbath or during early morning prayer time. A prophet, on the other hand, will pause to cock an ear to a low whisper snaking out to him from the depths of a darkened alley late at night, betting his life that it is God issuing the strange invitation. He knows that God is capable of this. A priest has God boxed in by predictable and unyielding systems of religion thought and practice (is not the very concept of "systematic theology" an oxymoron?) A prophet knows that God is dangerous.

For example, the Bible tells us about God ordering Hosea to marry a whore; Ezekiel to lie on his side for 390 days and cook bread using human waste; Jeremiah to invest in real estate in a city on the verge of being captured and destroyed. Then there was John eating locusts (forbidden food for a Jew); Jesus healing, eating and reinter-preting Sabbath injunctions, not to mention the people he hung out with. You know the rest.

A true prophet is God's extremist, a maximalist, with a willing-ness to go anywhere and do anything regardless of convention or personal concerns all for the sake of the mission. A prophet is driven by an inner burning message. A prophet has nothing to do with foretelling the future but all to do with explaining the present—as God sees it.

* * *

A few years back in Russia, I visited the city of Saratov, a city of roughly one million people on the banks of the Volga, about an hour-and-a-half drive from the border of the largest of the Central Asian Republics—Kazakhstan. Someone in that city had been writing to our denominational headquarters in Moscow for months asking for The Salvation Army to come to the city. This in itself was not unusual, in those heady days we got many such requests. The task fell to me to go and investigate. So I flew there one cold February night, armed with just the name of the person who was supposed to meet me.

It was a 10:30 pm when I stepped off the plane and there were two well-dressed men waiting for me. They carried mobile phones and they led me to a brand new, fully loaded Toyota jeep. If you have a cell phone and a brand new jeep in Russia that usually means you are "Mafiya" (In Russia the term "Mafiya" is an umbrella term loosely applied to anything from street level hoodlums to sophisti-cated organized crime operations). Things were getting interesting.

I soon realised that my hosts were pagans in every sense of the word, materialists with no sense of anything transcendent at all. As the jeep started up, our first conversation went like this:

"Geoff," said Evgeny, "do you want a cigarette?"

"No thanks, I don't smoke", I replied.

"Don't smoke, eh?"

"Nope."

(Pause) "Do you drink?"

"Nope."

"Women?"

"Only my wife"

(Pause) "Yeah, I've been thinking about giving up smoking too."

I spent four days being shown around the city by these men, and meeting with various people. They took me to a children's home run by the police, in reality a children's prison. Opened in 1837, it was still in operation. In this huge cavernous building the youngest child was six years old and the oldest 16. There were twelve-year-old girls who sold themselves on the highways to long-distance truckers, ten-year-old drug addicts, eight-year old thieves—and policemen were trying to look after them! I was shown into a room and told, "There used to be a church in this room in the last century, but we can't find anyone to come and do something. We need something for the kids that's lively, that's interesting." He was describing a Sunday-school program, without having seen one. "If you would like to come you can do this, you can do what you want", he said as we left.

Throughout those four days I was baffled as to why these two hoods were interested in hosting The Salvation Army. I tried subtly to let them know that even though I was a foreigner, I was not rich and if the Army came to town they were not going to get any money.

I must have said a hundred times, "We are not a business." But I sensed that they listened to me without really understanding.

The evening before I left, as I sat in an apartment on a white leather couch surrounded by expensive European appliances, I bluntly put it to them: "Evgeny, why have you invited The Salvation Army here? What interests do you have? What's in it for you?"

Something special happened at that moment. Jesus spoke to me through the mouth of a bandit. Evgeny, who I was sure had never, ever seen a Bible let alone read one, looked up into my eyes and said: "You know, I was in Moscow for a couple of years in the early 90's (pause). *I was in prison and you visited me* (pause), yeah, some little old lady from The Salvation Army visited me. So I said to myself, 'The Salvation Army is a good organization, when I get out I am going to do what I can to get The Salvation Army into my city'. That's why."

The question: Should we open The Salvation Army in this city at the request of the Mafiya? Would we be prophetic or not?

* * *

There is a fascinating episode from the life of Elijah in 1 Kings 17, in which the prophet heals the son of the widow of Zarephath by raising him from the dead. God sent Elijah to this woman in a foreign land that was in the midst of a famine—a strange invitation from a dangerous God. In a humbling act of submission Elijah moved in with the woman.

For Elijah, one of God's chosen people, to put himself at the mercy of a foreigner, a non-believer, was difficult enough. Compound this by the foreigner being a woman and a widow to boot, this was a real pride-breaker for the devout prophet. The gossip of the neighbours, the whiff of possible scandal, could not have sat well with the man of God.

I imagine that Elijah spoke much to the woman about his God, tried to evangelize her as we would say. There were several months of this with no apparent result. "What do you have against me, man of God? Did you come to remind me of my sin and kill my son?" was the question she flung at him on the death of her only child. She figured that her son's death was a punishment from God for her sins and that Elijah, as God's representative, was the harbinger of this punishment. She was trapped. He was obviously to blame but he was also the only hope she had.

Passionate person that he was, Elijah flung himself into the fray and onto the body of this young boy, raging against his death and against the hopelessness of the situation. No passive determinism here, no fatalistic, hand-wringing "if God wills". Elijah knew that it is never God's will that pain and suffering, injustice and sin have the last word.

A.W. Tozer wrote: "Many of us spoil our prayers by being too "dainty" with the Lord... We ask with the tacit understanding that the cost must be reasonable. After all, there is a limit to everything, and we do not want to be fanatical! We want the answer to be something added, not something taken away. We want nothing radical, and we want God to accommodate us at our convenience. Thus we attach a rider to every prayer, making it impossible for God to answer it. In a world like ours, courage is an indispensable virtue. The coward may snivel in his corner, but the brave man takes the prize. And in the kingdom of God, courage is as necessary as it is in the world. The timid soul is as pitiable on his knees as he is in society."

I imagine Elijah yelling, shouting at God, shaking his fist even in holy anger. How does a grown man cover a small boy? Hands on his hands, chest on his chest, feet on his feet, mouth on his mouth, as if to say, "Take my body, take my health, take my breath, take my life. Take it if you need it, but heal him, save him." Three times he did it as in the cumulative holy, holy, holy—fashioning a prayer out of pain, an act of worship, "kicking at the darkness until the daylight bled through" (in the words of a song by Bruce Cockburn).

The Scriptures say that if a Jew touches a dead person he is contaminated, made unclean. The boy was not only dead, he was a dead foreigner, doubly unclean one could say. A hot Eastern country and a body dead for a few days—the sight, the smell! How Elijah embraced this dead boy to his chest and breathed his breath into his fetid mouth without passing out, or worse, is something I will never know.

But none of that mattered. The instinct to save was too strong in Elijah, the different reality that blazed in his mind's eye rejected the evidence of his physical eyes. Charging through the religious, cultural and racial taboos, he would not let his religion, his race, culture, or his personal comfort stand in the way. He was, after all, a prophet.

After God brought the boy back to life, his mother said to Elijah, "Now I know that you are a man of God and that the word of the Lord from your mouth is the truth." "Now" is the operative word here. What Elijah had been saying for months made sense, came into focus. Now his reputation as a man of God had credibility, his God had been given credibility. Now the words he spoke were made truth, given weight and substance by his actions.

He had accepted the strange invitation of God and when the time came, was prepared to do what was needed, no matter how difficult and dangerous. The message needed to be given, the mission was all that mattered.

* * *

For the record, we did open up the work in Saratov, there is now a Salvation Army operating there and each week our team runs a Sunday-school type program for the kids in that children's home.

Many thanks to Jeff Lucas for his excellent book, Elijah: Stressed and Anointed *(Chariot Victor Bible Character Series, 1998). It is largely his thoughts on the prophet that I have reflected here and expanded on.*

Chapter 5: New World Fracture

THE IDEA OF THE COLLECTIVE IS CENTRAL TO RUSSIAN consciousness. The group has always taken precedence over the individual. Decisions are taken communally; things are done co-operatively. Bolshevism merely transmuted the mir, or village government, into the communist cell.

Before 1917, fear of the Tsar drew people together so that no one stood out to invite attention. It's the tall poppy syndrome. The communists understood this instinctively, and used it for their own ends. The people responded to the new regime in the usual way: they closed ranks and tightened the bonds of their life together. They helped each other to elude the system and to cheat it. Intellectuals met together by candlelight to discuss forbidden ideas and write poems with secret meanings. The aggressively capitalistic black economy flourised throught the years of socialism.

Then came perestroika, and everything changed. The West was admitted and it came in with a vengeance (and often in vengeance) with its money, its technology and, above all, its worldview. Men and women travelled over with a mission, to preach the gospel of the individual to a culture on the verge of disintegration through the steady erosion of its traditional social structures.

I never gave much thought to this Western idea of the individual before I came to Russia. There had never been anything to challenge it, no rival value to put it into perspective. But here it stood in conspicuous contrast to the surrounding culture. When I first arrived in Russia in the early 1990's, it was a rare and precious thing which the average Russian could not get enough of.

The winds of freedom blew strongly through the streets and people became drunk on the novelty as unimagined vistas opened up before them. They were sick of the sameness of Soviet life, sick of the collective—they wanted to experiment, to be out of the ordinary. They were being offered a feast after years of famine. Change was good; difference was better. Few at the time realized the price to be paid for this Faustian bargain.

In the years since perestroika, the flow of videos, books, records and people from the West increased to a flood that threatened to engulf the whole of Russian society.

Too late, it seemed, people lamented the loss of community and the triumph of the individual. Everyone started to complain about how rude the young are, how uncaring and violent, and how no one thinks of anyone but himself.

Neighbours who once shared hoarded food became suspicious of one other. The birthday parties with family and friends and the inevitable guitar, when folk songs were sung and stories told deep into the night has been supplanted by the video. Social drinking has become something more vicious. The sharp teeth of nationalism are bared as people insult and shoot each other for the sake of racial and religious differences. Read the signs, Jesus said, they will tell you that the end is coming. Without a sense of community, a society cannot last long.

Saddest of all is the fact that the Western Christians, and particularly we evangelicals who rushed in so eagerly when the Iron

Curtain lifted, are ourselves deeply infected with individualism. Like the missionaries who inadvertently carried diseases with them to the New World that exterminated whole races, we may have carried to Russia the germs of a gospel of the individual which may help to lay this society waste.

Chapter 6: The Community of God

WHERE I COME FROM, CHURCH IS A PART OF LIFE, BUT NOT the whole. IN the evangelical, subculture that birthed me, we knew our Bible enough to know that the church is people and not a building. Yes, the church is the people of God, not the place of God, although we always went to a place to see these people.

While church was not a place, it certainly had its place and knew its place, within our lives. And that is the point—within our lives. Because our lives belonged to us, and church, like many other things enhanced and enriched and complemented our lives, but it never became our lives, it never took over. We kept our lives, Christ's words to the contrary notwithstanding (Matthew 10:39). The matter was settled and unquestioned, more or less. Where I come from, that is.

Enter Russia, a land I lived and ministered in for nine years. A land where life is cheap and where the individual has never really come into the equation. Russia has always been a collective society, a land where community is understood and the common good—though often vicious and usually a defense against outsiders—takes precedence over all else.

In this century Russian Communism (as distinct from other variants) with its collective consciousness and social experimentation and mass demonstrations was just a new expression of the Russian soul—a soul that does things communally.

There are few tall poppies in Russia. The Reformation never got a peek in. Salvation never became as highly individualized and privatized as in Protestantism.

The Communism of the past 70 years was built on the Russian mentality of the collective, on a strong sense of community, and as such it was understood. But now those traditional communities, both good and bad, have been all but shattered. Disillusionment, economic hardship, materialism, nationalism, and post-modern individualism have booted down the door. I served in a bombsite of broken relationships resulting in a a loss of community and an increasing isolation of the individual.

In the vanguard of all that came streaming in from the West since perestroika, came the church in its multi-hued splendor. Divided in doctrine and practice, a squabbling and catty hydra of churches, para-churches and evangelical scalp-hunters, proclaiming unity in nothing but its commitment to disunity. Yet finding agreement in one thing—an unquestioned allegiance to the ideal of individualism. This has permeated almost all that has been said and done in God's name by evangelicals since Mr. Gorbachev first let us in. And so we have helped to hasten the demise of a society, inadvertently maybe, but steadily.

I see in the Bible a glittering hope in the community of believers, the people of God, the church, where believers lived and died and fellowshipped and ate and traveled together. Church was community and not an adjunct to an otherwise full life.

But when I rustled around in the bag I brought with me from

home and dug out my concept of church (I couldn't really find one of community) it seemed too amateurish, part-time, too safe, too inadequate. My church is stamped more with the radical individualism of Western thinkers like John Locke than the communal spirit of the first-century love feasts. What to say, what to do?

I needed to rethink church and family and community in Russia. The Scriptures, looked at through new eyes, pointed the way for me as I discovered a traditional God who spoke and acted in a traditional culture.

I said earlier that the church has its place within our lives. I have changed my mind on this, or Russia has changed it for me. The church must be our lives and our lives must have their place within the church, and not vice versa.

As I opened my home, my family, to our church in Russia, previous concepts of the same become more fluid and lost many of the sharp definitions that my Western upbringing had given them. I ended up no longer sure of where my family stopped and my church began. But that's all right. It is what was needed. With community becoming more eroded daily, the church needed to stand in the gap and become family and life to the people who join.

Russia taught me this: to follow the Jesus who said: 'Who are my mother and my brothers?' he asked. Then he looked at those seated in a circle around him and said, "Here are my mother and my brothers!'

Chapter 7: **Casualties**

"I had always believed that casualties must accompany any good thing, the better the thing, the higher the casualties"—Ward Just

GOD WILL NOT LOOK US OVER FOR MEDALS, BUT FOR SCARS. The apostle Paul boasted that he carried on his body the marks of Christ. But I suppose that most of us concentrate more on the medals than the scars. The medals that we sport are usually our more obvious victories: that outstanding convert, the growing church, the good sermon.

But what about the scars?

If, in the past, I did think of them at all, it was in a cavalier, macho way. In my mind's eye stood the old legionnaire at the end of the day—unbowed and firm, bleeding here and there, tunic torn, bloodied sword in hand, the knotty tissue of old scars livid amid the shocking scarlet of fresh wounds, with defiance blazing in his eyes. A rather romantic and unrealistic picture.

What I had failed to take into account, what I did not know, was how much the wounds would hurt; how much they would burn and sting, how the scar tissue would throb with a dull, incessant pain, how it would remain undimmed with the passage of time; how the layering of scars can kill the nerve-endings and cramp the joints and can make one bow low in pain and exhaustion, barely left with any will to resist.

One of the surprises of my years in church planting and church leadership has been the number of casualties among my own troops. Oh, I knew that there would be those who would fall away (the seed on stony soil and all that), but I cannot honestly recall anyone telling me just how skillful Satan would be. It was rumoured, but nothing much of a specific nature was said.

I suppose in my training days in Canada we concentrated, like many churches in the West, far more on evangelism than anything else. The battle at home rages outside the church, the challenge is how to get people to come to church, and then, once we manage to get them there, how to get them saved.

It happens rarely enough, so not a lot of thought is put into what should take place afterwards.

Upon being appointed to Russia I arrived thus deployed, and realised, not long after taking up my position facing the enemy, that the enemy was already past me, and I was holding the wrong weapons, in the wrong trench.

Getting people to come to church proved not much of a problem. Getting them 'saved' deceptively simple.

What next?

I had been trained as a commando, focused to parachute in, kick down the doors of spiritual apathy, deftly grab the sinner around the waist, and quickly back out of the room holding Satan and his minions at bay with my drawn sword—in and out like the a spiritual special forces soldier. But here I was, in and out of the room in a matter of spiritual micro-seconds, with the freed hostages on hand.

Salvation had occurred. Discipleship was now needed.

I was trained to swoop but what was now needed was that I lead a campaign. A long, long march through hostile territory which required that while I continue to swoop and fight battles, I also train and preserve my fighting force.

Well, the campaign got underway. The fighting was continuous. Reinforcements arrived, hostages liberated, trained and sent to the front. But the casualties continued to mount. The body count was high on both sides, and I must confess it took its toll on me.

Satan in front, coming head-on, I could handle. I was trained for that. I had on all the necessary armaments. But I learned that he rarely attacks head-on. He comes as a sniper. And what an unerring shot he turned out to be!

Each new year that the pilgrimage continued, that I led my troops on their campaign of faith and salvation through occupied and hostile territory, I noted the rising body count.

I was usually taken by surprise. Some were killed outright, shot through the heart so suddenly that the pain was sharp, but short At least it was over quickly.

Far worse, however, were those who were first wounded, to then die slow deaths that were agonising for the rest of us, and akin to murder for me.

Frantic efforts were made to resuscitate the wounded, while keeping one eye on 'damage control' (for the morale of the rest of the troops). I invariably ended up sitting and watching the seemingly inevitable death.

And then, all the guilt flooded in. He saved others-but he can't keep them! He can't save his own

Satan is a marksman.

He knew whom to pick off and how. The ones I never expected, the strongest, the most committed, the most talented and skilful, the ones I was closest to, the ones who, if you had asked me to point out my best soldiers, my most valuable warriors, I would have fingered them—these are the ones he started on.

Not all fell, but enough. Far too many.

I remember lying awake late one night, having so far spent the better part of it in bitter and impotent anger, shaking my fist at God and Satan and myself in turn.

We had lost another one—a true warrior; an evangelist who had brought scores to the corps; a leader in the church. A friend. Gone. Spiritually dead. Another casualty. No matter how hard we and the rest of the troops had tried, in the end it hadn't been enough.

The rearguard action had raged for about three months and I was exhausted. But worse, I knew that we had lost again.

It dawned on me that maybe because we sing so much about victory and triumph, we find it hard to acknowledge just how often Satan actually wins. Sure, the war is not in doubt - but it's the battles that take their toll. And no matter how many new engagements we win and even if the intake of new troops far out-weighed the casualties, still it hurts, and the scars remain-for life, as I now know.

Soldiers I have plenty of, but true warriors are rarer. They are harder to find. I will never have enough of them.

Now, as I rejoice over every battle won, and every new soul captured, I also carefully study the new penitents each Sunday.

I attentively scan the names of those preparing for membership and ministry.

I pore over the names in the church rolls and wonder and pray and worry.

I look with a more practised eye, more cautious, perhaps, praying that the Lord will guard my heart from hardness and cynicism, but also tempering my joy with a realism and healthy respect for the destructive capabilities of my adversary.

I know that some of them will fall, and some will desert.

And I also know that there is little I can do about it.

The casualties of war.

I now understand Paul when he cried out: "Besides everything else, I face daily the pressure of my concern for all the churches. Who is weak, and I do not feel weak? Who is led into sin, and I do not inwardly burn?" (2 Corinthians 11: 28,29).

I remember that Alexander the Great had to quit at 33 on the edge of India because his troops would not, could not, campaign any further.

I consider that this secret - of the need to continue the campaign might, in the end count, be one of the more valuable skills I can learn as a leader.

Chapter 8: Christmas in a Refugee Camp

I HELD IN MY ARMS A SMALL BABY, BARELY A WEEK OLD, BORN IN a basement under aerial bombardment and now living in an abandoned train wagon. He was a refugee like Jesus, a victim of war. He died a couple of weeks later in that same train wagon. His short life had never known peace. Did we fail him?

Another camp, another boy. He was a tow-headed blond, uncommon among such a dark people, though there are Chechens who will tell you that up to a third of their people are blond. He was very quiet with a preternatural stillness about him, unusual for a boy of his age. He was about 6 years old. Thin, with pale skin, he sat by his grandmother on her bed allowing her to caress him and run her fingers through his hair. He did not cuddle up to her in defense of our presence, nor did he crowd around us chirping for us to take his photo like the other children. He remained quiet and watchful, measuring us and taking little notice of the attentions of his grandmother.

'His mother is dead, killed in a bombing raid—a rocket got her,' the grandmother offered for our interest.

'Father?', I asked.

'Akh', she spat with disgust, waving her hand to somewhere out there.

'That means he's off with the fighters', one of our armed escort explained to me in a whisper.

We moved off into other areas of the large and overcrowded basement. Families had taken up residence everywhere, carving up the large space into separate units by hanging sheets and blankets. Homemade gas furnaces pumped heat into the rooms, blasting it into the concrete walls to creating a suffocating pall of humidity leaving the elders wheezing, the mothers flushed and the children coughing at night. The men were watchful and wary, keeping their distance and rarely offering the traditional greeting between menfolk in this part of the world. 'Asalaam Aleku!'

A collective of the mothers cornered us with their concerns about their children. As my companion listened sympathetically to their stories, I wandered back to our guards and found them in conversation with the blond boy who had now put on some old, torn boots and a grubby jacket and appearing out of the gloom, edged up to stand between them. He was talking weapons with them, unimpressed at Akhmed's choice of gun (a folding stock, short-barrelled AK-47 specially designed for special forces units). 'I have a machine gun at home. It's bigger than yours', he informed Akhmed and then went on to inquire about loading and firing procedures. He paid no attention to me—the foreigner—or to any of the other children who trailed me everywhere. He talked only with the soldiers.

We left the boy and moved out of the steaming darkness of the basement into the sharp sunlight and trudged through the thick mud stopping to visit other families squirreled away everywhere throughout the abandoned factory complex. Emerging outside from one small room that housed fifteen people sleeping in shifts, I saw that the boy had reappeared again.

'Where are your new boots?', inquired Ali looking at the old and torn shoes the boy was wearing. 'Our agency was here yesterday distributing new winter boots to everyone. I remember him.' Ali told me as an aside.

'I'm saving them', said the boy as he walked past us, shadowing the soldiers, certain of his future. I never did find out his name.

"Every warrior's boot used in battle and every garment rolled in blood will be destined for burning, will be fuel for the fire. For to us a child is born, to us a son is given, and the government will be on his shoulders. And he will be called... Prince of Peace. Of the increase of his government and peace there will be no end." (Isaiah 9:5-7)

Two thousand years since a small child was born in a barn and was heralded as the Prince of Peace. Are we any closer to the realization of that promise, has the Messiah truly saved us from ourselves, is there peace? Have we done all that we can do to make His Kingdom come, or are we among those who "dress the wound of my people as though it were not serious. 'Peace, peace,' they say, when there is no peace."?

Chapter 9:
Church? What Does She Mean to You?

"At every one of these concerts in England you will find rows of weary people who are there, not because they really like classical music, but because they think they ought to like it."
—George Bernard Shaw, *Man and Superman*

WILLIAM BLAKE, THE 17TH CENTURY ENGLISH ARTIST and romantic poet, was a visionary and a mystic and possibly a madman. He rebelled against all forms of earthly authority including the Church, but he loved God. In his poem, "The Little Vagabond", Blake wonders if people would more readily attend church, and enjoy it, if it bore a closer resemblance to the local pub.

Dear Mother, dear Mother, the Church is cold,
But the Ale-house is healthy and pleasant and warm:
Besides I can tell where I am use'd well.
Such usage in heaven will never do well.

But if at the Church they would give us some Ale,
And a pleasant fire, our souls to regale:
We'd sing and we'd pray all the live-long day:
Nor ever once wish from the Church to stray.

Then the Parson might preach and drink and sing,
And we'd be as happy as birds in the spring:
And modest dame Lurch, who is always at Church:
Would not have bandy children nor fasting nor birch.

And God like a father rejoicing to see,
His children as pleasant and happy as he
Would have no more quarrel with the Devil or the Barrel
But kiss him and give him both drink and apparel.

* * *

My wife and I are Salvation Army officers and served as church planters in Russia for nine years, from 1991-2000. At the opening service held for the Salvation Army in the southern city of Rostov-on-Don, one of our invited guests was the local Russian Baptist pastor. He was a cheerful, older man of great vigour who subsequently proved to be a good friend during our years in that city. He had a hard time with our service though and afterwards took me aside to give me a little "fatherly advice". The problem for him stemmed from the fact that our meeting had not been churchy enough. It had been "more like a nightclub than a church". I considered this a positive thing and told him so. "You see, Valentin Dmitrivich", I said, "people like going to nightclubs and don't much like going to church!" The point was lost on him, however.

Personally, I do not like going to church much either. I never have. I have gone through periods of relative enjoyment, but in the main, church has felt more of a chore than a pleasure—a drag as a kid and a duty as an adult. Admittedly this is a bit of a drawback, given my calling.

If I try to think objectively about the dominant feelings that have accompanied the word "church" it is sense of being trapped. Maybe it is the sitting down for long periods of time, I've always had a hard time doing this. Sometimes I just don't feel in the mood to be there. Sometimes I don't want to sing. Often I can't pray. When speaking as a guest at other churches, I can become agonizingly self-conscious, like an urchin in an upscale restaurant not sure of which fork to use. I want to run away most weeks. It is nothing to do with God, really. The issue is more with the hoops I am expected to jump through in order to connect with him.

Without a doubt, "church" is an overused word, especially in evangelical circles. Its definition has expanded to the point where it encompasses everything from a building, to an institution, to a home group. We can have both church architecture and a church without walls—the local church, the church universal and even aqua church. My kids refer to Sunday activities as going to "Hallelujah", a hang-over from our days in Russia when this universally understood word snagged their imaginations more than "church". Like the word "love" in popular usage, "church" effectively means most anything we want it to and consequently little that we need it to. Paradoxically, to be known and recognized as a church is a holy grail we pursue as evangelicals somehow thinking it will increase our appeal and acceptance in the world, while at the same time the term "church" engenders less than positive feelings amongst most of the unchurched populace.

Part of the problem is that as Protestants we have inherited an impoverished understanding of the church. The reactionary fervour of the Reformation had its down side and included in this was the lowering of expectations of what the church could be and should do. The practice of faith was moved from the communal to the individual, from the public sphere to the private closet and, in reducing the sacramental understanding of the church from seven to two, we also reduced the import and validity of what people expect to experience on a Sunday. The church, as the body of Christ on earth, is meant to be the place where our lives (of faith and lack of faith) are lived out together. It is a community in which we play out all the most significant events of our earthly lives and spiritual pilgrimages, a place to get married, be received into the body of Christ, confess our sins, be confirmed in our intention to live as followers of Jesus and prepare to enter eternity, among other things.

We have reduced the spell-binding mystery of union with God and each other through the irresistible seduction of the bride of Christ, to a cheery, Sunday morning therapy session where the main question put to newcomers is: "Did you like it?" (as if it were a meal at a restaurant or a newly released film). But surely the purpose of the Church is not to make people happy, but to make them holy, as Charles Colson points out in his book, *The Body*.

It has been my experience that the average Canadian evangelical has little or no idea that "church" is primarily a relationship in the context of a faith community. We have been enculturated to engage in programs and performance. Programs are clean, safe, efficient and excellent to hide behind. Relationships are costly and messy and demand an investment that spills beyond the walls of our church on a Sunday morning and that demands that we become vulnerable and admit our needs.

As Phil Needham points out in his book, *Community in Mission*: "The Church is not a grouping of individual Christians; it is a community in which Christians share in one another's struggles and hopes. In the fellowship of believers, Christians bear one another's burdens (Galatians 6:2), weep together, rejoice together (Romans 12:15), life one another up in prayer (Romans 1:9; 2 Corinthians 9: 14; Ephesians 1:16; Philippians 1:4; Colossians 4:2; etc), and love one another as Christ loved them (John 13:34). There is a togetherness in this fellowship that goes far deeper than mere camaraderie. The pledge which the Spirit empowers the Church to carry out is the pledge of members of the community of faith to be with one another in every circumstance."

The church I am involved with now is in the inner-city neighbourhood of Regent Park, in the downtown core of Toronto. It is a poor and rough neighbourhood. Our faith community can seem at times like anti-church. It is actually a bit of a mess most Sundays. A spectacularly chaotic sprawl of adults, children and things. A shaggy mongrel of a "church", cobbled together with donated equipment, wounded people and cash infusions from our head office. It is not recognizable church for most people who have been taught otherwise but it does mostly contain what I do like about church, though, and that is the people. They come seeking other people, nosing out the possibility of human warmth and the touch of another human being, the promise of a well-fed belly and some bright, emotionally charged singing that allows a brief forgetting of the monotony of daily life. And of course the chance that Jesus might show up. It's a bit of a gamble, but Jesus usually does show up. Not in response to any summoning or conjuring, not because we have played and sung so hard that the emotional pitch is high and hot enough, but because he wants to. Because he promised that "where two or three are gathered", because he inhabits the praises of his people, because he also lives in our part of town.

And so our people come to church each week. Troops returning from the front of their daily existence, sporting fresh wounds, fatalities as common as mud. Our people, our church—with blackened hearts many of them, battered personalities and bruised consciences, scarred in body and mind and will and spirit. In Psalm 24, David claims that that only those with clean hands and pure hearts, only those who have not lifted their souls to idols or sworn deceitfully, only such righteous people will receive the Lord's blessing. If this is the case, then we haven't a hope at our church. Here there are few clean hands, few pure hearts, plenty of idolators and deceitfulness abounds. But they come, we come, just the same, "bending under heavy loads; loads of injustice, of resentment and hate, of suffering and sin... dragging the world behind them, with everything rusted, twisted, badly adjusted." (Michel Quoist)

We lift our hands in praise, stained and disfigured by sin like leper's stumps. We pray, often with speech slurred by the drunkenness of our compulsions and marred by the curses that our lives seem to be on that particular day. We talk and hug and fellowship together even as the sharks of mistrust and envy, hatred and lust swim between and around us. We listen to God's word, sometimes without comprehension, hardly hearing through our pain and dysfunction. But sometimes like Peter stepping out of the boat and fixing our eyes straight ahead, trying not to look down at the raging waters because we know it is the difference between getting to Jesus or drowning in our circumstances. And like a kid searching for Waldo, we look around and crane our necks, looking for Jesus, wondering in whom he will show up this week. Such is church as we understand it—definitely more hospital for sinners than museum for saints. A bit like the local pub, actually, not a recognizable program in sight. And this I can handle, most weeks.

And you? What does "church" mean to you?

Chapter 10: A Form of Godliness

"Romans help Romans, Hebrews help Hebrews, Africans help Africans, but the Christians help everyone."
—A pagan priest explaining the sudden explosion of Christianity to a Roman governor

"...the gospel does not require converts to leave their people and join another people... people like to become Christians without crossing racial, linguistic, or class barriers."
—Dr. Donald McGavran, *Church Growth expert*

WE'VE GOT HISPANIC CHURCHES AND ASIAN CHURCHES and Black churches, we got all kinds of churches... you know what I'm going to do? I'm going to go back to Mississippi and start me a white church! That would upset everybody!"

The preacher thundered from the pulpit in the auditorium of Asbury College in Kentucky. Harsh words delivered with conviction and a trace of anger, or exasperation, crowding the edges. The preacher was black, the congregation mostly white.

Dr. John Perkins knows what he's talking about and his credibility and experience make him almost untouchable. He can say what he really thinks and there are few who would challenge him. Over seventy-one years of age with a grade three education and honorary doctorates from seven universities, Dr. Johnson beares on his body scars from the civil rights wars in the States. He knew Martin Luther King, mentored Jesse Jackson and is consulted by US Presidents on matters pertaining to race. The Doctor travels about three weeks out of every month from his home base in Jackson, Mississippi where he heads up the John M. Perkins Foundation for Reconciliation and Development.

After chapel, Dr. Perkins talked with me further about his convictions and vision. "The Christian church is to represent a new nation on earth—instead we accommodate racism and bigotry. Ethnic churches are a heresy that nullify the power of the Gospel. Why did Rwanda happen, why did Liberia happen—supposedly Christian countries, priests and pastors chopping people up with machetes—how could that happen? Because we had a Christianity stripped of the true power of the Gospel, a form of godliness but without the power of the Gospel to reconcile peoples to God and to their brothers and sisters".

The core of Dr. Perkin's message is a conviction that the Gospel allows no room for mono-ethnic, culturally-based churches. That in fact, to create and sustain such expressions of church and faith are to deny the essence of the Gospel message. He is not alone in his thinking.

Ken Shigematsu, an Alliance pastor from Vancouver, speaking at an Intentionally Multicultural Churches Conference in Toronto, said much the same thing. Ken, an ethnic Japanese, seems almost the opposite of the grizzled John Perkins. He is young and attractive with a good sense of humour. But his message is no less unequivocable.

"The early church clashed over this issue—Peter and Paul went head-to-head on this one. Was one ethnic group to be given priority or are all on equal footing before God (Galatians 2:11-21)? Unfortunately our people want to feel as safe as possible while hearing a dangerous message (the Gospel). But it is wrong to tamper with the nature of the Gospel even if your motivation is to reach more people. In a world divided, God has called us to the ministry of reconciliation (2 Corinthians 5:13-20)."

Daniel Diakanwa, a Congoleise, is on the staff of the Cross-cultural Ministries Department for the Salvation Army in the New York. Daniel wrote a book, *Key to Intercultural Ministries: A Biblical Perspective on Human Reconciliation*. In it he said: "Encouraging the separation of church congregations by race ethnicity or social status, whether consciously or unconsciously, would defeat the purpose of Christ's mission in earth... Christians should not dare to challenge the secular world and its distorted moral values with the gospel of love and reconciliation, while remaining unreconciled with one another and indifferent to the sin of segregation between God's people."

Is there any Biblical support for mono-ethnic, culturally based churches? Not really, in fact there seems to be rather clear direction that churches, as outposts of the Kingdom of God, should model the kingdom values of inclusive fellowship, where all tribes and nations gather to worship, where the divisions between Jew and Greek, slave and free, male and female, rich and poor are cause for celebration and not rationale for segregation. "My house will be called a house of prayer for all nations", God reminds us in his Word.

If praxis alone is the measurement we wish to employ then we should have some concerns too. Is it good strategy for any denomination to continue to plan and plant ethnic corps as viable expressions of church community? A number of large, ethnic church congregations in Toronto are starting to lose their second-generation. "The problem with culturally-based churches", another church leader explained to me, "is that they are non-sustainable. You may get the parents, but the kids are Canadians. They are going to local schools, listening to MuchMusic, hanging out in the malls. Where do you go from there?"

Assimilation, immediate or gradual, is an inevitability for immigrants, in multicultural Canada no less than melting-pot America. Consequently such expressions inevitably lose their raison d'etre, gradually weakening with each successive generation. In marketing terms, they have a built-in shelf life, are non-sustainable in the long-run and non-renewable.

More disturbing must be the theological implications of continuing to promote such models. In a world caught in a giant tug-of-war between globalism and tribalism, endemic with racism, ethnic and religious strife, what message should the church be speaking? What should the church in Canada be saying to a nation where, over the next decade, we will welcome 375,000 immigrants per year?

The sharp end of the stick may evidence itself more brazenly in a Bosnia or a Rwanda than in Canada where thankfully we prefer to settle our differences in ways other than mass genocide. But the benignity of our context should not lull us into thinking that our methods are right.

Thinking back through Dr. Perkins sermon, I understood that he was saying that we reveal ourselves and our prejudices regardless of how hard we try to seem inclusive. It occured to me that were I to announce to my denomination that I felt led to plant a Caucasian congregation in Toronto I would be not only refused the opportunity but likely be hauled in to have my head examined—and quite rightly too! Don't get me wrong—I have no interest in planting a whites-only church, I'm just not sure we should be planting other ethnic, racially-based churches either. The difference, at the end of the day, seems rather academic.

A few concluding thoughts from Dr. Perkins. "Power, power, power—everything in the church is about power these days. Another fad, another gimmick, another distraction from the Gospel. Another Gospel. I have a friend who is an Indian and a philospher and a Christian. You know what he told me? He said that everything that a Benny Hinn or an Oral Roberts or any other healer, miracle-making, prosperity preacher can do, he can take me to a village in India a find local holy man who can do the same thing—everything. (Pause) Everything except one thing—there's one thing the holy men can't do. They can't make a high-caste Indian love a low-caste Indian. That takes the power of the Gospel!"

.

.

Chapter 11: The First Family

OUR ELDEST ADOPTED SON, SERGEI, IS RUSSIAN. HIS MOTHER and father died in a house fire when he was five. After the fire, his other half-brothers and half-sisters were sent to orphanages. Sergei was not admitted anywhere because he is HIV positive. A local doctor took pity on him allowing Sergei to live in the children's wing of the city hospital.

When he was seven, Sergei came to stay with us for a summer to attend our children's camp. My wife, Sandra, and I were childless then and couldn't make up our minds whether we wanted children or not. We had no intention of adopting. After the summer, however, Sergei stayed on with us and eventually joined the family.

At this time, our "family" was fairly fluid. Many different people lived in our home at various times. The supper table was always an eclectic mix of whoever happened to be in the area. Most of the ladies at our church had a far better idea of what food supplies might be in our cupboards or fridge at any given time than either my wife or myself. "Church activities" often took place at "home" and "family days" were usually spent at "church" (in whatever building we had managed to rent at the time). We had no beds in the house, only pull-out couches to maximize sleeping spaces. Every "family" meal became a sacrament in its deepest sense.

One day on a train trip from Moscow to Rostov, Sergei decided to sketch a picture of his family. He drew a big house with about 25 windows. In each window he drew a face. When asked what he had drawn, he explained that this was his family. He pointed to each face and named the person it represented—each one was a different member of the church. He wasn't trying to be clever or profound; he was describing his reality.

* * *

Recently I was in a prayer group with some other pastors. One of the younger couples, not long out of Bible College and expecting their first child, shared some needs from their church, then finished with a request for prayer for the impending birth of their first child. "Of course, after the birth, the baby will become our first priority, before our ministry," they said.

This clarification, or declaration, was accepted, judging by the nodding of heads and general encouragement that was offered from everyone present, myself excepted.

Why did this innocuous and seemingly normal comment catch me? After all, nothing was said that was not in keeping with conventional wisdom in evangelical circles regarding the place and function of the home and family. First God, then my family, then my ministry—this is the triumvirate of priorities to which most of us subscribe. It was taught to me when I was in ministry training and was modelled by the evangelical climate in which I was raised. Dr James Dobson's books and videos were everywhere, encouraging us to "focus on the family."

But looking hard at what little the Bible actually says concerning the nuclear family unit raises a few questions. Jesus, for example, makes three direct references to the nuclear family unit in Matthew 10:34-39, Matthew 12:46-50 and Luke 9:57-62. None of them would encourage my young friend much. A cruise through the Old Testament is even bleaker. It is difficult to find one nuclear family unit that would not be described as dysfunctional by today's evangelical standards.

Jesus' life and teaching tell us that marriage and family should take a back seat to the "universal proclamation of God's salvation and the formation of a new 'first family'—a world-wide Kingdom-building company, in which membership depends not at all on bloodlines, but on faith in the Messiah" (Mary Stewart Van Leeuwen, *Gender & Grace: Love, Work and Parenting in a Changing World*). He demands that his disciples place marriage and family second to their allegiance to him, his Kingdom and mission.

Author Rodney Clapp writes: "For the Christian, church is First Family. The biological family, though still valuable and esteemed, is Second Family. Husbands, wives, sons and daughters are brothers and sisters in the church first and most importantly—secondly they are spouses, parents, or siblings to one another."

The "God-then-family-then-ministry" paradigm likely owes more to our cultural values than it does to Kingdom principles, especially our Western, middle-class, predominantly white, cultural values. We have romanticized the idea of the "traditional family" to the point of idolatry. Jesus tells us that the order should be God followed by mission. Everything else—family, home, work, etc.—finds its meaning and place within these imperatives.

Somewhere along the line, around the mid 1950s I reckon, North American society came up with an idealized version of the nuclear family that closely reflected the values of most Christians.

As secular culture became increasingly hostile to the Judeo-Christian worldview, the family became the bulwark against "the world." As Christian values gradually lost their influence over virtually every area of public life and culture, we concentrated our efforts on protecting the family. Theologically, we encouraged an individualized faith which, while "evangelical" in deed, was privatized and compartmentalized in kind.

Evangelical rhetoric on the importance of family stresses that "a Christian home should be an... oasis far from the maddening throng and godless currents and pressures... the last bastion against depersonalization and dehumanization... the basic institution which undergirds all else... Only through the family can we hope to achieve security, a sense of well-being and belonging... If the family fails, then all other institutions of society will fail" (Van Leeuwen).

This exaltation of the family unit has extended to encompass the home as well. We eventually came to see our houses as fortresses to protect the sanctity of our families, places to retreat to after work or study, to shut out the pernicious influences and incessant needs of a sinful and broken world, to recoup our strength and nurture our families. A safe place where we jealously guard our "private time" and our "personal space."

My first ministry appointment was to the First Nations community of Gitwinksihlkw in northern Bristish Columbia. This is where my doubts really took off. The Nisga'a people came from a tribal/clan tradition where, historically, children were raised in lodges according to tribes (Eagle, Raven, Wolf or Killer Whale) that were determined matriarchally. The tribal unit was predominantly considered family and home, not the nuclear/biological unit. This has changed over the years and the Nisga'a now live in houses in a semblance of biological family units. Children, however, are still very much communally raised. Although our time in the village lasted only ten months, I never did figure out who most of the children belonged to biologically.

My education continued in Russia. Multi-generational families had little concern for privacy and virtually no concept of personal space. Hospitality was a way of life and not an extra effort. These were hallmarks of the Eastern-Oriental home and family life, indigenous to Russia (and to Jesus, a first-century, Palestinian Jew). My cultural assumptions on family and home were challenged at every level.

I realized that there are many different ways to *do* family, and many uses for the home. The norm that I grew up with and that was presented as the Biblical ideal is not that at all. It is not necessarily a bad model, but it is the minority model in a world context. It certainly does not carry any particular Biblical authority.

Are we missing something that God wants us to reconsider? What if, instead of trying to save our families and our homes, and in the process losing them (statistically, divorce, incest, youth delinquency seem to be more or less the same regardless of whether a family is Christian or not, thereby validating Christ's words in Matthew 10:39), we would be willing to lose them for the sake of mission, for the cause of Christ?

When was the last time you invited someone home for a meal from your church on a Sunday? What if the borders of our family were not rigid but fluid, allowing the inclusion of others, not simply as guests but as... family?

What if our homes were changed from fortresses into hospitals and mission centres? There are thousands of Christians in Canada who have a spare bedroom in their house. At the very least most of us have far more space in our homes than is considered normal (or decent) in most countries and cultures in the world. What about sharing that space? What about seeing your home as a mission centre? If every evangelical Christian living in Toronto took in one homeless person, the homeless problem would be solved.

What if our children and our houses turned out to be God's secret weapon for impacting our communities and reaching the lost?

It seems to be what God had in mind.

For further thinking on this subject see Mary Stewart Van Leeuwen's book: Gender & Grace: Love, Work and Parenting in a Changing World, *IVP, 1990.*

Chapter 12: A Picture of Jesus

From the ministry of a friend of mine (visit to a private residence):
"As I knocked on the door of the apartment I prayed: 'God I don't know the man behind this door. What I do know is that he's gay and that he needs to experience your love. Help me to love this man.' I was somewhat taken aback by the flamboyant figure who greeted me as the door opened. He invited me in and seemed thrilled to see me—thrilled to see anyone. Minutes into the conversation, he looked at me and said: "I have experienced nothing but hate and bigotry from the church for over 40 years. Why should I trust you?' This was my moment. 'I did not come here to judge you, but to show you Jesus Christ. Your issues with God are between you and him. I'm here to be a friend to you.'"

* * *

AND SOMEWHERE THEREIN LIES THE CRUX OF THE DIFFICULT and complex relationship between the gay and evangelical community. It a fairly lengthy history marked largely by misunderstanding and uninformed assumptions, scapegoating and cowardice, fear, secretiveness, bigotry and just plain obtuseness. On both sides.

Back in the late 80's things got quite heated for a while, apparently sparked by an editorial in my denomination's otherwise tame official publication. Somehow the issue in question fell into the hands of the less-than-tolerant people at *Xtra!*, Toronto's gay flagship newspaper. The guys and gals at *Xtra!* went crazy and started printing all sorts of incendiary nonsense in an effort to rally their community to do something about us (The Salvation Army) and the evangelical community in general. I even got into the act, living as I did in TO's gay village at the time, and wrote some letters to *Xtra!* daring them to have the courage to publish my rather arrogant and naïve missives. Understandably, nothing I sent in was ever published.

The Salvation Army bobbed and weaved its way through the issue until the gay resistance settled down to an annual boycott of our Christmas fundraising efforts, still in effect. There are periodic breaches of the ceasefire as in 1992 when the then Toronto Mayor refused to allow the Army use of the City Hall Square for our annual Red Shield kick off due to our "discriminatory policies". Matters settled down to a surly hostility, a mutual wariness and distaste.

I cannot really speak about the rest of the country but know that in Toronto the relationship between "us" and "them" is strained, to say the least. To be really blunt, "they" hate "us", and I'm not too sure but that it might be reciprocal. Our opinion of each other has been long decided and neither side seems willing to make any revisions. Or maybe it is not so much unwillingness as an uncertainty, a confusion.

We have worked hard at our local church to gain access to local schools in order to help in relationship building with children in our neighbourhood and to raise our profile, weaving us into the fabric of community life in our "parish". One of the junior highs has denied us access because they have several openly gay teachers on staff who would be "uncomfortable" in allowing a "homophobic organization" such direct access to their charges.

Inflammatory rhetoric seems to be de rigeur—"they" have their propaganda and we have "ours". Never mind that our human rights and religious freedoms are being trampled on and that we could have cried foul for discrimination based on religious beliefs; never mind that our distinct lack of homophobia is displayed through the hundreds of gay men and women who received assistance in numerous forms from The Salvation Army on a daily basis and that no one has ever been refused help due to their sexual orientation or lifestyle. Never mind all that. In this particular theatre perception is reality and that perception is usually crafted by others.

It cuts both ways, unfortunately. Lest we get too self-righteous and feel that we alone are the victims, a quick cruise of the website www.godhatesfags.com should shame into silence anyone bearing the tag of evangelical. We too share a burden of guilt.

So, what is to be done? This is a question we have been wrestling with in our church since our inception. Toronto contains the third largest gay population in North America after San Francisco and New York. They have a high public profile (Pride Day celebrations every June draw more visitors to Toronto than any other single event from across the world, bring several million dollars into city coffers and is endorsed and attended by the Mayor and other public figures) as well as huge political clout (of the three MPs representing the Rosedale-Centre political riding in downtown Toronto—municipal, provincial, federal—two are gay). And yet gays remain possibly the most hurting, lonely and misunderstood sub-culture within our society. And the last place most of them would ever think of turning to is the church, particularly an evangelical church.

At our church we have made tentative forays into accessing the downtown gay community but it is hard going and very confusing for "them" and "us". Fear and mistrust are the most common emotions. Defensiveness and hostility permeates everything it seems.

The problem for we evangelicals as Biblical Christians who hold to an essentially fundamentalist (I know, I know—a loaded term!) view of the Bible and God and sin and salvation and all the rest is that our usual mission praxis kind of falls apart here. The typically applied "hate the sin, love the sinner" has been rendered inoperable by the gay community. We can take such a position with alcoholics and addicts, with criminals, prostitutes, with almost any particular constituency mainly because we can separate the person from the sin that they have embraced. I mean few people are going to argue us that alcoholism is a positive thing or an alternate lifestyle, right?

Within the gay community, disentanglement of the sin and sinner is not possible—they have made it so deliberately. Acceptance of the sinner (as we have tried to do) means necessarily acceptance of their sin (which we cannot do) as they define themselves and find their identity in this orientation and the subsequent—inevitable—actions it produces. According to the doctrine of the gay lobby, orientation without action is not possible, if a person is gay he or she will engage in homosexual acts. Orientation is defined by action based on that orientation. Therefore our evangelical construct is not understood and completely rejected. It renders dialogue, let alone relationship, all but impossible.

So we are at an impasse. To accept a gay man or a lesbian woman is to accept their lifestyle, condone it and affirm it as right. For most of us this would mean a compromise of principle as Biblical

Christians. Yet the call is there, the pull toward a constituency of people whose fear and distrust and lostness is so evident in spite of their surface brashness and brazen overcompensation. Engage with a member of the gay community—whether it be a leather-clad muscleboy in a downtown coffeeshop, an old queen in a shabby rooming house, a tattooed lesbian on fightnight at a local boxing club or a former pastor in his meticulously kept apartment on a cold winter evening, and the unease is there. Always.

All else aside, what this does mean is that a degree of intelligence and even sophistication needs to be applied toward mission in this context. A level of skill, of craft, well-honed with deep thought and breadth of knowledge and understanding that is so often lacking in our mission endeavours. We need to approach engagement with the gay community with the same degree of commitment and preparation as we would apologetics or ethics or world religions. It is a complex issue and in fact, is not even one issue, but many.

We must be prepared to understand and accept that there will be people who are interested in the Gospel and those uninterested. That some people we will attract to Jesus and others we won't even interest. We need to be prepared to understand that there are openly gay men and women who identify themselves with Christ and consider themselves Christians. The disagreement here will be in interpretation of Biblical injunctions and we may just have to agree to disagree. Heretics to be combated? Or hurting, broken people trying somehow to find a peace with God, however incomplete?

The answer is to focus not on the sin but on Jesus. Sounds simple, but once we understand—I mean really understand—the realization that we cannot convert anyone, that in fact this is the job of the Holy Spirit (to convict and convert), then a way opens. Our job is simply to show them a picture of Jesus. As a friend of mine says, to "place people in the way of God's grace by virtue of my encounter with them trusting the Holy Spirit within me". It is about reconciliation and love, aspects of God's plan that he has entrusted to us (2 Corinthians 5:16-21), and not condemnation and judgement which he has reserved as his exclusive purview (John 5:19-23).

How hard it is for us not to name sin and go after it. We want to identify it and define it and shape it to cover people's lives and cloak their actions like ill-fitting hairshirts. But at the end of the day, the issue is God's identity and not ours, God's love and forgiveness and grace toward God's children and God's efforts to reach down to them—to us. He has far less need of our zealous defense of him than we think.

Jesus was considered a traitorous outcast for his embrace of societal misfits and blatant sinners whether they were tax collectors, prostitutes, non-Jews, heretics, whatever. As he walked amongst these people, supped with them, accepted them as his friends, even partied with them, noticeable things happened.

Firstly, his censure by the religious establishment was almost total and unanimous. Secondly, the broken people he hung out with became transformed in his presence. Rarely, if ever, was Jesus proactive in naming their sin and in detailing what steps were needed to get things sorted.

People seemed to know they were sinners already. What they needed was a strong acceptance in order to have the courage and faith to make the changes they all along wanted to—Zaccheus, Matthew, the woman at the well. Jesus' inclusive acceptance and attractive holiness called out to the best in people. Being in Jesus' presence, seeing him, having a relationship with him, was enough to move them toward God and toward wholeness. So there is an imperative for us to be, more than to do.

* * *

SCENE TWO: From the ministry of a friend of mine (visit to Metropolitan Community Church—Canada's premier gay and lesbian congregation): "I entered through a locked door that led to their office area. I met the receptionist, a lady in her 50's. I was wearing my uniform jacket and as I spoke I could see that she could not take her eyes off the patch on the front left breast area patch (which incorporates the Salvation Army's Red Shield). I explained the purpose of my visit. Skeptically she said: 'The symbol on your jacket represents homophobia.' I explained: 'We're not all like that and I am sorry people have represented themselves that way. For us this symbol represents reconciliation for people to God and to each other. Its about showing people God's love.' She gave me the most peculiar stare. Later as I exited the building I could hear her speaking behind my back to another person: 'Come here—look at that! He is Salvation Army and he isn't anything like what you would think they are.'"

Chapter 13: Why Should the Devil Have All the Good Parties?

"To confront the Empire is not to fight against it but to live beyond it."—Seminar leader at Messiah College, May 2002

"Because we love something else more than this world, we love even this world better than those who know no other."
—C.S. Lewis

IT IS SAID THAT CONFESSION IS GOOD FOR THE SOUL, SO... HERE it goes. I celebrate Halloween! It's true, I allow my kids to dress up and go out trick or treating. I carve pumpkins and buy candies to give out to children who come to our door in their spooky costumes. Now having so declared myself, allow me to offer a reasonable defense before the collective wrath of my fellow evangelicals descends upon my head (or at the very least, piles up in my mailbox).

Halloween is one of those sub-cultural shifts that caught me unawares upon my return from Russia. Having grown up in a relatively strict (by today's standards) evangelical—some would say fundamentalist—home meant that there were many things that were not allowed. To be fair, my parents loosened up as the years passed and my younger sister and brother had less restrictions to skirt than myself and my older brother. But in the early years, we rarely went to the movies, we categorically could not play any card games, on Sundays we were not allowed to play outside or with friends, TV was rationed and certain shows were off-limits, make-up (for girls) was not encouraged... I could go on. These and other things defined the parameters of our world as shaped by our faith and our understanding of Christian practice. The parameters were designed to keep us on the straight and narrow, protected from the corrupting influences of the world, to separate us really. Such was the world that most of my evangelical peers grew up in in the 60's and early 70's. It was pretty much the same for all of us.

Looking back now, it seems like there were a lot of rules and taboos. Some quite helpful actually, while others were rather silly and often unwittingly producing the exact opposite outcome than originally intended (for example, as a small boy I came to dread Sundays, particularly in the summer, and so developed an aversion to church services that—believe it or not—plagues me to this day). We were products of our times though, and I don't blame my parents or feel any deep seated resentment for any of these things. They were doing the best they could and the results are not bad if I look at how we all turned out. The point is, however, that Halloween was never taboo back then. Everyone I knew celebrated Halloween—even everyone in our denomination. It never even crossed our minds, as far as I can remember, that it might be a bad thing to do.

Sometime in the late 1980's or early 1990's, it seems that Halloween came to the attention of the ideologues of evangelical culture in North America and was put on the "hit list". Being out of the loop for about a decade in Russia (where Halloween is not celebrated—nor incidentally is it much celebrated anywhere else in Europe. Having said that, England celebrates Guy Fawkes Day which is infinitely more macabre and disturbing than anything I've ever seen during Halloween), I was blindsided by this shift when I found myself back in Canada in the autumn of 2000. As October approached, the question being asked was a hesitant, sussing out of one's position: "How do you feel about Halloween?" Not knowing that I was supposed to feel a certain way about Halloween, my ready admittance of complicity in the celebration got me into a fair few scrapes. I understood quickly enough that Halloween was something evangelicals—and particularly charismatics, who seemed increasingly to make up my acquaintances and friends—no longer did and that any mention of Halloween inevitably led me into arcane and rather confusing discussions on the occult, satanic ritual abuse, druids, generational curses, African voodoo and rock music, to name a few.

Looking back I realize that all the while these card playing, movie going, DVD owning, pierced-ear, evangelicals blithely went about activities that would have almost certainly consigned them to at least purgatory (had we believed in it) if not the fires of hell itself a few short years ago, while at the same time they were castigating me for my observance of a celebration that was one of the annual highlights of my early years. I smelt the whiff of cultural Christianity at work and decided to look a little deeper into the whole matter.

Finding credible information about the origins of this festival has proved harder than I thought. There are plenty of Christian ministries via the web that offered their take on the celebration. Some of this stuff is quite detailed, but the more I read, the more suspicious I became. My natural tendency toward dialecticalism aside, I soon found myself at sea amid an ocean of unsubstantiated charges, unprovable facts, unverified assertions, decontextualized Scripture verses and that odd mixture of sweeping generalization allied with minute and unnecessary detail that I have found to be a good indicator of falsehood afoot. A heavy reliance on anecdotal evidence also does little to further one's argument.

How certain brothers and sisters have made discoveries that no other historian or anthropologist have been yet able to figure out (such as, the origins and purpose of Stonehenge) or come into possession of certain facts that the FBI has no knowledge of (ie, "Occult killings take place in the U.S. every Halloween") mystifies me. Needless to say, I found this search inconclusive and not overly helpful.

In the end the issue is far deeper than whether or not one dresses up and goes trick or treating on October 31. It is a fundamental approach to mission and living as a Christian in a post-Christian culture. My celebration of Halloween and the good Christian men and women of the opposition represent differing concepts of engaging with culture and society. The issue is engagement versus withdrawal and where one draws the line. When does the prophetic cross the line into compromise?

Jesus advised his disciples (being the sheep they were, about to be sent out among the wolves) that the real trick (pardon the pun) was to be "in, but not of" the world. A tremendously difficult balancing act. I own a painting that I purchased in Madrid some years back from a sidewalk artist outside the Prado. It is a mixed medium piece using oils and sand. It is of a very vulnerable man (he is naked) rendered virtually as a stick figure, and hence fragile and easily broken. He is wearing a halo which marks him, in my mind, as a saint. He is balancing precariously on a tightrope stretched over flames, the flames of hell, I figure. I saw something of myself in that painting which is why I bought it and why it hangs over my bed. I also see it as the preferred "missionary position" (believing that all believers are to be engaged in mission, hence we are all missionaries)—having the courage to walk that razor's edge, fully aware of one's own vulnerability and brokenness, yet keeping on in the midst of that surrounding, threatening danger.

The other "position" seems to have little of the missionary about it and takes it cue from Paul's admonishment in 2 Corinthians 6: 17, usually taken out of context and rendered most typically in the King James Version: "Wherefore come out from among them, and be ye separate, saith the Lord, and touch not the unclean thing; and I will receive you." The intent is withdrawal rather than engagement, the point of relation to "the world" is an adversarial one, primarily defensive ("keep oneself unspotted") and hence reactionary.

It is to me an odd sort of theology best exemplified by the old Protestant believers I encountered in Russia. Under Communist rule things were so bleak and unrelentingly hostile, that theology took a heavenward turn. There was not much to look forward to here on earth, so the trick was to get saved and then grit your teeth and hold onto your salvation until you made it to heaven (achieved in a number of ways but mainly through extreme legalism and a sharply defined dualism of sacred and secular that was applied down to the minutae of daily existence). Fully two-thirds of the songs in the Russian Baptist Hymnal are about heaven. Apocalyptic themes, the longing for Christ's return, obsession with *the world*—all staple fare for sermons on any given Sunday. Given the circumstances in Russia prior to perestroika, this is understandable and the courage and suffering that these brothers and sisters endured demands our respect and admiration. To construct such a worldview here, however, is unwarranted and a bit freakish. There are Christians who sit inside their homes with all the lights off on Halloween night, refusing to answer the doorbell and open their door to the halloweeners.

I look at it this way. I'm not too sure how the holiday came about. I think that All Hallows Eve is when the forces of light and darkness engaged in battle and the good guys win and hence the following day is All Saints Day. Whether this was a pagan ceremony coopted by the Church and *sanctified* for holy purposes or syncretized in the interests of compromise, well—it beats me. As it stands today, it is what it is. Whether Satan and his minions need a particular day in order to practice their dark arts, it seems somewhat like imposing the same time-space construct that we as humans are forced to live with on beings and forces that live in another dimension and I'm not sure this is a valid understanding. I don't give October 31 as a particular night much more credit than I do April Fools day (most fools seem pretty active to me all year around) or Easter even—I take the celebration of the remembrance of the crucifixion and resurrection as deadly serious but that fact that it changes date from year to year would suggest to me that the value is in the *how* of the observance and not particularly the *when*.

As for all the pagan trappings that represent the "thin end of the wedge", well, how far back does one start this wedge? Christmas Trees—ever looked into the origins of that? Santa Claus? Rearrange the letters and he becomes Satan Claus! Easter? The word comes from Esthe, who was an ancient Germanic, wood goddess. What about the days of the week? In case you're wondering, they come mostly from Norse mythology (Wednesday = Wodin, Thursday = Thor, Friday = Frida... you get the picture). The symbolism of mystical and magical figures? Well I grew up on C.S. Lewis' *The Lion, the Witch and the Wardrobe*, as many of us did. Tolkein, of *Lord of the Rings* fame was a Christian and a mentor to Lewis. One of the best sermons I ever heard was on the fairy tale of Snow White as a resurrection metaphor. "Do you believe in magic...?", goes the song. I am afraid I do.

Besides, if everyone around me is celebrating something, I want in. I'm going to get in on the action and see what cracks of opportunity appear. To ignore it is a denial of reality that is not prophetic but may actually border on the delusional. To run away belies Paul assertion to the Hebrew Christians: "But we are not of those who shrink back and are destroyed..." (Hebrews 10:39). Why should the Devil have all the good music? Why should the Devil have all the good parties? Same principle, I reckon. He stole it all from God (and us) first—so why let him keep it?

So my kids dress up. Not as witches or murderers or devils—why would they? The bad guys are the losers after all and my kids want to be on the winning side. So they choose a superhero, they become angels, crimefighters, knights, good guys. They go out to party and get candy. I send them out to be "in, but not of". Then I sit at home and wait for all the opportunities about to come to my door. Last year 290 of them came knocking.

Our house straddles the line between the housing project of Regent Park and the upwardly mobile, gentrified Cabbagetown neighbourhood. Sixty-five percent of Regent Park's approximately 16,000 residents are 18 or under. The kids from Regent don't trick or treat in the Park. They head north into Cabbagetown where the houses (and money) are. At the north end of Parliament Street is St. Jamestown, a complex of low-rent and subsidized apartment housing around 11,000 people, most of whom are new Canadians, almost forty percent are Tamil. They head south to Cabbagetown on Halloween. As one beleagured resident grumbled goodnaturedly to me: "The Tamils attack from the North and the Regent Parkers from the South."

The whole world came to my house last Halloween. Every conceivable nationality, big kids, little kids, kids in costumes and kids without costumes, kids I knew and kids who were complete strangers. We prepared packets of candy, invitations to our Saturday Kid's Church and glossy evangelistic booklets obtained from Child Evangelism Fellowship. I heard a Somalian girl tell her Chinese friend as they passed by on the street: "Go there—that's the house where you get the Jesus books!"

So, what shall we wear this Halloween?

"Any man's death diminishes me, because I am involved in Mankind." —John Donne

I GUESS IT ALL STARTED WITH THE DEATH OF PRINCESS DI. I remember that morning well, a friend called me with the news, quite upset. The subsequent media coverage and very public mourning, the eulogies, the creeping beatification... at first it all surprised me, then I became fascinated and eventually irked. Surely if ever there was a case of a saint being simply "a dead sinner revised and edited." (in the words Ambrose Bierce)—this was it. I never was one of the Princess' fans and rarely thought about her. When the popular press did bring her to my attention though and I paused to reflect, I couldn't say she was one of my favourite people. Her death struck me as sad and somewhat tawdry, kind of like her life—of little significance in the greater scheme of things. Obviously I was in the minority.

What I really remember about that week was another death—that of Mother Teresa. It was bad timing on her part, though. The media, given the choice between an old Nun and a young Princess, went for the Princess hands down. We, the public, predictably followed.

I mean how can you compare the two? On the one hand a wrinkled, old slum-dwelling Catholic nun from Albania with a sharp tongue and an inflexible moral code versus a young, vibrant, saucy princess who danced her nights away in clubs and on yachts and stuck her tongue out at her stuffy in-laws. One loss was more acutely felt than the other and hence the subdued references to Mother Teresa's quiet passing while the endless outpouring of grief, the songs, the fields of flowers for the Princess' spectacular exit.

On the surface Princess Di possessed all the qualities our society values and desires—youth, beauty, romance and glamour. The reality was actually a rather shallow, self-centred woman who spend her nights clubbing with a succession of lovers, chalked up a broken marriage and seemed an indifferent mother to her two sons. She didn't have a job, contributed little to society and even her much-vaunted charitable efforts constituted about one quarter of what the average society matron undertakes in any given year. But she had become in life an icon, a "Candle in the Wind" and in death, "the People's Princess", the media-shaped perception transcending the reality of her life.

Mother Teresa was from a place no one had ever heard of, was old (an unforgiveable sin in our youth-obsessed culture) and she spent her nights in the fetid slums of Calcutta nursing human refuse from the streets and alleyways. Age and wrinkles, faith, a foreign accent and a distinct lack of glamour conspired together to lessen the Mother's star value. The press needed more to work with and we the public needed more to hold our wandering attention.

It's not very hard to see why we valued Princess Di more than Mother Teresa, in life and in death and why their passings produced such disparate reactions.

* * *

I thought about the Princess and the Nun again a couple of summers ago. The neighbourhood I live in went through a rough spring and summer with shootings almost monthly—all of them fatal and all of them young men in their late teens or early twenties. The assumption is that they are drug and gang related (although its anyone's guess as almost three years later, no one has been arrested and not one of the seven murders solved).

Two of the men were shot in the same night. One was a drug addict, no one special, just another "crack-head" in a part of town that has hundreds of them. He was shot in the head. His body was found on a grassy triangle just up the street and across the road from my office early one Sunday morning. Rumour has it that he owed money to some dealers.

The second boy was shot several blocks north of our neighbourhood. He was a few years younger than the first boy but also shot in the head. This boy, however, had a brother playing in the NBA and he himself was a rising basketball star, maybe slated for the big leagues and with a scholarship in pocket to an American university that autumn.

The death of the first boy got one paragraph in our city's largest newspaper the following day and no further mention that I could find. The second boy's death was front page news, the subject of editorials calling for justice and denouncing the "shameful waste" of such talent and such promise. His mother was interviewed ("he was always a good boy"), his brother came back from the U.S. ("he fell in with the wrong crowd") and the usual community leaders weighed in ("How long, O Lord, how long?"). His funeral made the front page again a few days later with a second flurry of editorials and opinion pieces and political posturing regarding at-risk youth, cleaning up the ghetto, the evils of drugs and the perniciousness of systemic racism.

While both deaths were shameful and tragic wastes, there was a difference. Boy one was no rising star and showed no particular talent or potential. But I also happen to know that the boy two was no angel either. He not so much fell in with the wrong crowd as much as he was the wrong crowd. Whether his mother or brother or the community leaders or editorialists knew it—he was rumoured to have robbed people and he sported an attitude that on the streets brings trouble as surely as blood in water attracts sharks. I asked one dealer from our neighbourhood about him. The laconic answer was "that boy messed with a lot of people." As much an explanation for what happened to him as one will get in these parts.

This is not to say that I think he deserved what happened to him. Few people deserve a bullet in the head. But ... I digress. What struck me again was the value we assign life and the loss of life based on whether or not that life or those lives embody qualities or abilities or sustain fantasies that we value and affirm. In the case of the second boy it was his athletic potential and in this sports-crazy culture that is indeed a valuable commodity (my neighbourhood tends not to breed either Mother Teresas or Princess Dis).

So the city mourned the Athlete and paid little attention to the death of the Addict.

* * *

Fast forward a few months to the tragedy of September 11. I guess I'd better say up front that I was as shocked and saddened as anyone by the death of those 3000 plus people and the bewildering pain carried by their families and friends. By and large, I support the subsequent course of action taken by the U.S. and I am most definitely not a member of that angry and unimaginative chorus of finger-waggers who blame U.S. foreign policy for the attacks and feel that this somehow creates a balance of justifiable blame between America and the terrorists. Having thus qualified myself ...

I thought hard of the thousands of Americans who died at Ground Zero and watched with a deep interest how, in the subsequent days of rage, the condemnation poured in and support gathered from the international community for retaliation to ensure that justice was served. A historically unprecedented coalition of nations (of varied and competing political systems, philosophical and religious convictions) joined forces to ensure that the outrage of so many murders did not go unanswered.

And yet, and yet... I also couldn't stop thinking about the Princess and the Nun and the Athlete and the Addict. Something niggled at me, something more than the knee-jerk reaction of a contrarian.

What if the dead had not been Americans? What if the attack had not been levelled against the most powerful nation on earth? What if it had taken place elsewhere, in, Dakar or Lima or Brazzaville for example? Would it have mattered as much? Would anything even remotely like what has taken place in the world since September 11, taken place? Would anyone have cared enough?

My mind wandered back a few years to Bhopal, India. Remember Bhopal? In the middle of the night on December 3, 1984, over 40 tons of Methyl Isocyanate and other lethal gasses leaked from the (American corporation) Union Carbide's pesticide factory in the city of Bhopal, India. 8,000 people died immediately and over 500,000 suffered from injuries. Ten to 15 people continue to die every month from exposure related complications. The current death toll is well over 16,000. The evidence points to corporate negligence—a drive toward profits at the cost of worker and community safety.

Did the world change on December 3, 1984? Not really. There was no international coalition formed, no retribution paid, no justice served and no official blame laid. But just as many grieving spouses, parentless children, childless parents as at Ground Zero—more even. No, September 11, 2001 was the day the world changed as we are reminded contantly. I pondered on...

The Gulf War. In response to aggression against another country, America went to war and in a dazzling display of techological superiority wiped out, in a few weeks, over 100,000 Iraqi soldiers. American losses were just over 40 (and not all of those combat related). The 100,000 doesn't include civilian casualties from the bombing campaign. 100,000 versus 44! 100,000 versus 3,000? I couldn't help myself, I thought on...

There are 13 million AIDS orphans presently living in sub-Saharan Africa whose numbers will balloon to 40 million by mid-century? Presumably this represents 26 million dead parents, soon to be 80 million. Give or take a few hundred thousand. Will the world change then, once this number is reached?

There are approximately 40,000 children who every day die of starvation and hunger-related conditions (diarrhea, dehydration, etc.) and whose individual lives could be saved by a postage stamp's worth of food?

There are tens of thousands who die daily from diseases that could be cured by immunizations that would cost developed countries approximately 0.24% of their GNP?

I heard the other day a conservative estimate that there were 4,000 civilian casualties in Afghanistan due to the carpet-bombing carried out in retaliation for September 11. Al-Quaeda and Taliban members aside, this surely makes things about even, right?

I could go on but we've heard it all before, read the statistics, watched the emotionally-charged infomercials on TV. Nothing new here, nothing we don't know. But still the question for me: why are some lives valued more than others and how is this determination made? Is it a geographical thing, a matter of where one lives? Or maybe something racial—dependent on skin colour? Or cultural, linguistic, economic... what? How does the math get done?

The reality is we do assign differing value when people die and if we do this in death, do we do it in life. In viewing people and their worth through the eyes of our culture and through the lens of its value system we are forced to conclude that some people must be simply worth more than other people.

Chapter 15: Scandal as Mission

"Be it true or false, what is said about men often has as much influence upon their lives, and especially upon their destinies, as what they do."
—Victor Hugo, *Les Miserables*

"You see, we have no reputation to lose."
—William Booth

A FRIEND OF MINE WHO IS FAIRLY WELL KNOWN IN EVANGELIcal circles in this country, told me of an incident from his younger days when he was in training down in Chicago. It was late at night and he was in a bar talking with some prostitutes and pimps. The police busted the place and my friend was rounded up along with the other patrons, handcuffed and led away to the paddy wagon. At the police station he protested: "But, I'm a pastor!"

Looking at his long-hair and beard, jeans and single earring, the booking officer retorted: "Oh yeah? Well, what's a pastor doing in a place like that?

"Can you think of a better place for a pastor to be?" he replied. They let him go.

* * *

On Friday nights a small group of people head out from our church offices to prayerwalk in our community. Sometimes this means walking the neighbourhood praying, sometimes just talking to people as they sit outside and taking prayer requests or praying on the spot and sometimes going into local bars and restaurants to pray and talk with folks. Late one night two of our pray-ers were in a restaurant in the heart of Regent Park when the place was raided by the police looking for weapons.

Suddenly eight policemen with riot guns crowded into the small restaurant. A female officer approached Rob (the ministry coordinator at our church) first. She asked if he had a gun to which he replied "no". His innocent, babyface apparently failed to convince her. Grabbing the front of his shirt she hauled him to his feet rather roughly and proceeded to frisk him. The jacket he had on with the small red Salvation Army shield embroidered on the front and the large, eight-inch high red Salvation Army shield emblazoned across his back made no difference.

No weapons were found and the police eventually left. Rob was immediately congratulated, his back was slapped, he was "in". The other patrons of the restaurant thought it hugely amusing that the Salvation Army had been nailed by the police. We had been treated in the same way they felt they were usually treated at the hands of the authorities.

Rob better understands now what it feels like to be stereotyped and powerless and at the mercy of a system that can act on assumptions and often denies justice to those at the margins. He's the better for what happened and so is his ministry. He has "friends" at that restaurant.

Then there was the time when my wife was mistaken for a

prostitute. She was standing in front of the fortified Hells Angel's clubhouse just east of our neighbourhood and even though she was in full Salvation Army uniform, including her jacket with the large red shield on her back, she was "cruised".

"Want a ride?" the prospective "date" asked as he drew his car up to curbside.

"No", Sandra replied

"C'mon—it'll be fun!"

"I have enough fun in my life", accompanied her withering glare that I as her husband know only too well. He got the message and slithered off doubtless to continue his hunt elsewhere.

Then there was the time I was driving in my car and had just pulled away from our offices when I spied one of the local working girls waving me down. She wanted to ask a few questions about her boyfriend. He was due to get out of prison soon and wanted to get into a drug program. I pulled the car over and rolled down the window. The girl bent down and put her head through the passenger window and we talked. Just then a police car pulled around the corner coming to an abrupt stop, in the middle of the street.

Had I been in my Salvation Army uniform all would have been fine. My protestations that I was a minister, that I knew this girl, that I worked in that building, that this was "business", were all met with gruff skepticism. I'm a good talker though and eventually he let me drive off without any charges or without recording my license number. I'm not sure why he let me go. From his perspective it must have looked all bad. Maybe it was the originality of my explanation that got me off the hook, maybe it had been a long day and he couldn't be bothered, maybe ...who knows? What I do remember is the contempt in his voice and the disgust in his eyes as he watched me drive off.

Then there was the lady who attends our church who came to me one Sunday with a message from her son. He told her to tell me to be careful at night. I had been walking through the Park a couple of Friday nights previous (actually it turns out that it wasn't me but some of our other church members) on one of our prayer walks.

The three prayerwalkers came near to where some drug dealers were doing some business. They were all carrying guns. One of them noticed our guys first and reaching for his gun murmured to the others: "Who are those white boys?" Another dealer who I know, squinted through the night, saw our jackets, thought he recognized me and said: "Its OK—its the Salvation Army. That's 'my boy' Geoff—he's cool". The prayerwalkers passed quite oblivious to the situation they had almost stumbled into.

* * *

I don't really remember when I was first informed that henceforth in life I was to be judged by the company I kept, by my friends. I think it was by my mother and likely during one of the much dreaded Mom-Dad-Son talks that inevitably occurred immediately following parent-teacher interviews at whatever school I was attending at that time in whatever city The Salvation Army had appointed us to. These talks punctuated my formative years with a dreary and dreaded regularity.

Why do you hang around with those people? You have nothing in common with them. They're dragging you down. They are a bad influence. Endlessly it went on—or so it seemed at the time.

My only defence (when I offered one) was a long shot at comparing myself to Jesus who was also, I earnestly pointed out, a "friend of sinners". Nobody bought it though. The difference of course—as my parents invariably countered—was that the people Jesus hung out with changed for the better because of his influence on them.

All my youthful spin-doctoring aside, there is something to this whole thing. Can you tell a person by the company they keep? What does it say about that person? And if so, I often wonder what people do say of us?

I know of one minister, fresh back from the anti-globalization barricades in Quebec City in 2001 where he fought—actually fought—against what he perceived as injustice, oppression and other things contrary to his faith and understanding of God. Now this guy is likely involved in all sorts of scandalous causes, making a nuisance of himself all over the place, using his denomination and his calling as a man of God in order to annoy, confuse and anger the powers that be. A prophet or just a pain?

We forget that Christianity was born in scandal and that Christ was born at the centre of a scandal, to a young, unwed mother in a patriarchal society that valued women little enough. We forget that this scandal dogged him his whole life (Matthew 13:55). We overlook that in his three years of active ministry Jesus scandalized and shocked, through word and deed, on virtually a daily basis. We forget that Christianity continued to be a scandal until Constantine co-opted us into his empire.

The word scandal comes from the Greek word *skandalon*. Skandalon occurs 15 times in the New Testament. Depending on the context it means either a "stumbling-block" (three times), an "occasion of stumbling" (once), an "occasion to fall" (once), an "offence" (nine times) or "things that offend" (once). Twice it is used in direct reference to Christ, in Romans 9:32 and 1 Peter 2:8. Christ the Scandal—an offence to some, a Saviour to others.

The Salvation Army was nothing if not a scandal back in its youth. In order to fight the "white slave trade", an industry whereby thousands of underage girls from Britain were sold into brothels throughout Europe, our second-in-command (Bramwell Booth) and W.T. Stead, (editor of the Pall Mall Gazette) actually had a young Salvationist work her way undercover into a brothel posing as a prostitute in order to get information? They then went so far as to actually buy a young, underage girl—in order to make their case? Things got violent and ugly. It went to trial with Bramwell, then second in command of the worldwide Salvation Army, in the dock after being transported to court in a police wagon and sitting locked in a cell until the trial each day. There were mob scenes. "Can the Salvation Army's status survive a scandal which was now headline news across the globe?", wondered one observer. The papers had a field day. Such a thing would never happen in today's Salvation Army.

"Everybody has settled it that we are fools, if not a great deal worse; therefore we can go into a town and do exactly what we think best, without taking the least notice of what anybody may say or wish. We have only to please God and get the people saved, and that is easily done." Booth once said by way of explaining his success.

Well, this certainly was the case during my years of ministry in Russia. A fool? Possibly. A great deal worse? Definitely! Looking back now I realize that throughout my nine years I there I was constantly in trouble with local authorities and the official church structure. Considered disreputable, fanatical and dangerous, I have been publicly denounced by a vice-mayor as "an especially dangerous agent of the CIA"; Shouted at by a Russian Orthodox priest for my apparent complicity in the sack of Constantinople in 1453 and then dismissed with the admonition that due to my status as a leader the only Biblical directive relevant to me was Matthew 18: 6,7. I have been denounced countless times in newspapers—both local and national—wherein I have been accused of everything from stealing children, drugging them and shipping them off into slavery in the West, to practicing the black mass as a Satanist, to being (my personal favourite) a "spiritual bandit". I have been threatened by police, kicked out of buildings and out of cities, investigated by federal prosecutors, mocked and ridiculed, ripped off, lied to, screamed at, received death threats, had property and vehicles stolen and vandalized, mail opened, phone conversations tapped, I've been shot at and eventually barred from re-entering the country as persona non grata. I guess you could say I was a bit of a scandal myself.

And yet, we always got along really well with regular folks in Russia, the people in the market place, the petty criminals. Once after our offices in Rostov-on-Don had been robbed the local mafia put word out that resulted in a complete return of every last thing that was stolen. A drunk who vandalized our van one night in St. Petersburg was brought, a little worse for wear, to our door late one night at gunpoint by a couple of the local hoods who wanted to know what we wanted done with him (our merciful approach appeared to confuse them somewhat—different concepts of justice I concluded). I have known grown men—tough, hard Muslims—staying up all night outside the room where I was sleeping, playing poker to stay awake, in order to guard me from being kidnapped.

But what a relief to come home to Canada where everyone loves us. My Salvation Army uniform gets me into places I never dreamed of being. I've even joined a service club. I am courted because of what I represent. People keep telling me how wonderful the organization

I belong to is and what wonderful work we do and when they find out about our church and where it is and what we are trying to do, well, the admiration and affirmation knows no bounds (but from a distance, of course, always from a distance).

But you know what? I'm not really all that sure I want their friendship. Don't get me wrong, a return to those "Russian battles" is not something I long for. And I do not wish to court conflict or even to deliberately offend. It's just that I fear I might compromise my mission, if not my faith, by who I'm seen with.

You see, the lines have to be drawn somewhere. And in a neighbourhod like mine, the lines are drawn fairly clearly. Were I to become, say, a police chaplain like a number of my fellow pastors and don a police uniform from time to time, carry a badge and spend a lot of time with the local police and in the local police station—it would impact my ministry negatively. I would not be trusted in my community or among my people and I would lose the relationships I have formed with those who most need what I think I have to offer them. Sure, it would mean I would no longer be suspected of frequenting prostitutes and my staff would likely not get roughed up in bars. But it also might mean that a Friday night encounter with the dealers could turn out much different. Down here one is definitely judged by one's friends.

I hope we are doing what Jesus would do, ministering "outside the camp, bearing the disgrace he bore." (Hebrews 13:13). I hope the attitude we get at times is in the same vein as what Jesus had to put up. "Why does your Teacher eat with tax collectors and sinners?" I think I am justified in spinning it thus this time around, more justified than I was as a 13-year old academic misfit trying to rationalize my misbehaviour.

"Go to the lost, confused people right here n the neighbourhood. Tell them that the kingdom is here. Bring health to the sick. Raise the dead. Touch the untouchables. Kick out the demons... This is hazardous work I'm assigning you. You're going to be like sheep running through a wolf pack... Some people will impugn your motives, others will smear your reputation—just because you believe in me. Don't be upset when they haul you before the civil authorities." (Matthew 10, *The Message*)

Chapter 16:
There Goes the Neighbourhood!

"The Word became flesh and moved into the neighbourhood."
—John 1:14, *The Message*

MUCH HAS BEEN SPOKEN AND MILLIONS OF WORDS written on how one should plant churches. Manuals have been produced and are being produced, seminars attended videos watched and cassettes listened to; the gurus and planters push their models and tell their success stories for us to consider. Resources galore to help us do what we need to do. Curiously though, little is ever said about the where of planting. This is because all of the above is predicated from an assumption that all players are working from the same page, that there is consensus and agreement and that it can be taken for granted that we all understand that we plant in those areas that we ourselves feel at home in.

We plant in those areas where we feel most comfortable—among people that look, think, act and talk like ourselves. Staying in one's comfort zone where it is easier to navigate is seen as common sense and even good mission practice. It is effective and after all "one can't argue with success" (another assumption here, by the way, that we all accept the same definitions of success). Thus expediency becomes the bottom line. In a results-oriented, corporate culture driven by consumerism and materialism we define effectiveness by prevailing cultural norms. And in so doing, we have taken a sociological reality and made it a mission strategy. How else to explain the homogeneous principle of church growth, for example? Biblical values are about changing the habits of people and the rules of society and calling us to a better—although more difficult—standard and value system. Just because something works, does not make it right.

Given the fairly consistent and rather unequivocal words of the prophets with regard to social and economic justice; given the life of Jesus who kicks off his whole active ministry by getting up in a synagogue and reading Isaiah 61:1,2 and then sitting down (thereby basically saying "I've just told you the important stuff about who I am"). Who then goes on for three years to hang out with the working poor, prostitutes, national traitors, unsavoury racial types, religious heretics and terrorists. Given the record of the early church, mainly composed of "the slaves and politically powerless peoples of the first- and second-century Roman Empire, among whom Christianity had its most extensive appeal" (Phil Needham, *Community in Mission*).

I reckon that John White said it best almost twenty years ago, in his book, *Flirting with the World.* "Meanwhile our churches, like secular associations, are concerned with fund-raising, beautiful buildings, large numbers, comforting sermons from highly qualified preachers, while they display indifference to the poor, and to the pariahs of society—drunks, whores, homosexuals, the poor, the insane, the lonely. Jesus himself would find no place in our all-too-respectable churches, for he did not come to help the righteous but to bring sinners to repentance. Our churches are not equipped to do that sort of thing."

One of Jesus' best praxis on mission was slipped in at the beginning of the Sermon on the Mount. Matthew 5:13-16 introduces the subsequently overused metaphors of salt and light. The Church popularized these images as evangelism taglines to tell us what we should be. But the metaphor has as much to say about where we should be, as it does about who we should be as the people of God.

Where? As "light", in the darkest places (not much point in lighting a candle either in a well-lit room or in a room where there are other candles already burning) and as "salt", in those places most in danger of spoiling and going rotten. The kicker at the end about "good deeds", I understand this as confirming a redemptive theology of salvation, of asserting that social action *is* evangelism.

As we strategized and pioneered in Russia, the implications of this led us into some very dark and rotten places, from the drug-infested streets of the southern village of Kuleshovka (known as far away as Moscow for its drug problem) to the war-torn region of Chechnya. Its not that we had no other choices and not that there were no relatively nice places wanting a Salvation Army presence in Russia. Rather it was that as Christians we had formulated our mission in the context of who we were called to be in the body of Christ and through our relatively straightforward reading of the Bible. It seemed like a no-brainer at the time. It still does.

So, why the erroneous assumption about the role of place in evangelical church planting strategy?

At the end of the day I think there are two reasons, one personal and the other corporate. Personally, I have come to understand that we are unwilling to submit ourselves, our lives, our possessions, our children, our time, to the greater need of a mission imperative. We understand our faith and service as an aspect of our lives and not a whole-life passion; we have decided that accomodation to the prevailing culture is more desirable than counter-cultural, incarnational ministry. Consider it the "sacramentalization of our faith" (read as reducing a worldview to a ritual).

Put more simply—we do not want to live in those houses in those places, we don't want those people to be our neighbours, we don't our children to go to those schools. We don't want to lose our lives, so we save them and being saved ourselves, think that this allows us to in turn save others (like us) as we act out mission from our security and strength and talents, instead of out of our weakness and brokenness and powerlessness. And the dominant church culture tells us in no uncertain terms that we can, and even should, do this. That, in fact, it would be counter-productive and ineffective to do otherwise. It would not produce the desired results if we did. We would not be successful and failure is our culture's one unforgiveable sin.

The second reason is corporate and it has to do with money. All roads lead to the money men in today's Church, it seems so often. Undoubtedly it does take money—and a lot of it—to engage in mission. Saving the world is an expensive proposition. However, once any organization—particularly if that organization is the church—allows their accountants to shape mission policy and control mission strategy, there will be problems. Financial people, by the very nature of their skill-set, are generally conservatives and true mission is a risky business. Any faith institution lives with an inherent tension between the money people who will work to enforce risk-management and the missioners, usually the risk-takers. This can be a creative tension to ensure wise stewardship of God's resources—creative and healthy. But it is the kiss of death when these parts of our structure are allowed in the driver's seat.

It is not financially good sense to open churches in impoverished areas among people with few financial resources. Ghetto churches don't pay for themselves, is what everybody understands—so why go there? It will cost too much, use up too much of our present resources. The returns will be minimal and the success, if it comes at all, too hard won. It is bad business.

I guess the question we have to ask ourselves is if these reasons of ours are good theology or just good sociology. What is a successful church and what price is too high to achieve that success? Where would Jesus live in Canada, who would he hang out with, where would he go to church?

* Names have been changed

NOT A FESTIVE SEASON GOES BY THAT I DON'T THINK ABOUT THAT EVENING over twenty years ago now. Not to mention the two other guys I spent it with. Christmas Eve 1982. The memory flares briefly every year, like the embers of a dying fire caught by a passing breeze. Three lives that converged for a few hours one night.

It was Floyd's idea. He was the main man, after all. A well known person in this particular part of town. A smart guy who had gone to College, who read the financial section of the paper and who spoke quietly and politely at all times. He also dealt drugs to all and sundry. The sort of very unofficial community leader of dubious reputation and motive that this part of the city regularly produces through a process of natural selection.

I had become acquainted with Floyd through his younger sister Molly. We were dating. Molly was a great girl, even if her brother was the biggest dealer in the area and her Mom's house a nightly "whos who" of the old Cabbagetown underworld. Molly was a tomboy who could fight like a guy, play billiards with the best, had freckles and red hair and a smile of compelling charm. It was a bit of a stretch for me to be seeing her (being who I was). It was maybe even more of a stretch for her to enter my culture (for many of the same reasons). But we had formed an odd alliance, were hopelessly in love with a teenage intensity, and wonderingly explored each other's worlds as we sought to learn about each other. Her mom liked that she was seeing "a good, Salvation Army boy". My parents, God bless them, smiled and accepted with some concern. My grandmother muttered darkly in the background about Irish Catholics.

Anyway, it was Floyd's idea to do something for the poorest kids in the neighbourhood for Christmas. His plan was to get a list from a contact he had in the local welfare office, a list of the absolutely poorest of the poor. We would take them gifts on Christmas eve, just like Santa Claus and his elves. I would provide the van and wear my uniform to give it some legitimacy with the officialdom. Floyd would dress up like an elf (he was physically rather small, like a lot of big men). For Santa Claus, Floyd enlisted his friend Mickey. They were friends in that they had grown up together and I think Mickey ocasionally worked for Floyd. Mickey was generally acknowledged to be the toughest guy in the neighbourhood. A big, brawler with rock-hard muscles, shaven head and a menacing scowl on his face. Kids in the neighbourhood usually spoke his name with an accompanying glance over their shoulder, just in case. Such was our Santa.

The three of us gathered late afternoon on Christmas Eve. I drove up in our church van, borrowed for the occasion and packed to the roof with toys, selected and purchased by the drug dealer. I hopped out of the van and smiled as I looked Floyd up and down. He was dressed in a green elf suit complete with a fur-trimmed, pom-pommed hat and pointy slipper-shoes. He was dwarfed (or "elved", maybe) beside Mickey as Santa Claus—his red cap pushed back from his massive brow and a cigarette stuck in the side of his mouth. I wanted to laugh. But then realized they were looking me up and down in my Salvation Army uniform—my shapeless, blue accountants' coat, my policeman-like cap perched on my head as my ears slowly hardened and froze, my knotted tie... Floyd and Mickey had a point—who was I to laugh? We all nodded and accepted the inevitable neccessity of what needed to be done to get the job done.

So off we went winding our way through the maze of buildings that comprise north and south Regent Park.Through the stairwells with walls blackened from cigarette lighters and into beaten, metal elevators smelling sickly sweet of government disinfectant and urine. Floyd smiling, Mickey swearing, myself silent. We didn't really talk much to each other. Men usually don't when engaged in a demanding task.

I remember one door that opened slowly to a small, thin black girl. In hindsight things are always remembered bigger than they are, but I still remember her as small. Little more than a dirty undershirt topped by huge, inquiring eyes, about 5 years old. The apartment behind her was dark and devoid of any Christmas ornamentation, but we could hear loud music and the grating laughter of drunken adults. Once the door was open and she spied Santa Claus, well, her wide eyes got even wider (if that was possible). Mickey rose to the occasion and "ho-ho-hoed" with gusto. Floyd presented her with her toy—a doll, of course—which she clutched excitedly to her thin chest before slipping quickly back into the darkness without uttering a word, leaving the door to shut on its own. No adults ever appeared. Mickey lit up another cigarette, swore again and looked more threatening than usual. Floyd smiled in his cynical, satisfied way. I said nothing, just shook my head. This scene was repeated throughout the evening.

As we walked through the entranceway to one high-rise, a gang of local lads huddled around the warm entranceway shot a few mocking insults towards us, Santa Claus in particular. Mickey pulled his Santa beard down around his chin and filled the chill air with something other than good tidings. Recognizing that Santa did exist and that he was actually none other than who he was, the toughs paled and skittered off. Floyd laughed to himself while Mickey looked disappointed. I brought up the rear with my ears just about frozen off.

And so we got through the evening. Close to a hundred toys we gave out. We covered the whole of the Park. We felt pretty good. Even Santa had visibly softened by the end of the evening. We shook hands and the elf and his Santa wandered off to their women. I went home to my parents to catch the tail-end of our family Christmas Eve celebrations. I never saw Mickey again and Floyd only a few times. Molly and I broke up the next spring and our lives moved on in their predetermined courses. Christmases came and went, accumulating with the passing years.

A few years years later, I bumped into some guys I knew from the Park and asking after old acquaintances, learned something about my Christmas companions. Floyd was eventually arrested and did a stretch in prison. It changed everything—like a butterfly with its wings manhandled by an excited child. His inviolability had been breached. He came out a wreck and lost everything—his house in the swank Beaches neighbourhood, his wife. The careful, yet fragile facade of respectability he had constructed around his essential lawlessness had broken apart at the seams. The last anyone heard he was reclusive presence, seeing no one, possibly addicted himself. But who really cared? There were new players in the neighbourhood, new drugs too.

As for Mickey, he went drinking one night with his best friend. One drink led to another, one comment to another, an argument flared and Mickey's infamous temper exploded. There is really no delicate way to put this... pouring a can of gasoline over his friend, he set him on fire and killed him. His time in prison is to be considerably longer than Floyd's was.

And so every year as Christmas approaches I find my thoughts returning to that evening, almost in spite of myself. Trying to make sense, I suppose, of what happened then and subsequently. To all three of us. As each successive year passed, I would take out the memory, dust it off, turn it around in my head, shake it like a bottle that won't open and attempt to extract something redeemable. Then put it away again for another year and get on with the busy reality that is Christmas in the Salvation Army. The memories fade a bit with each successive year, but this ghost of Christmas past visits me annually.

Then I came back to the Park, appointed to live and work in the neighbourhood after twenty years. The place has changed a lot. I've changed a lot. But sometimes, the more things change the more they stay the same. Regent Park is worse in some ways than it was then. The drugs of the 80's have given way to Crack. The fists and knives and baseball bats of past decades have more and more given way to guns. The pasty faces of generational white poverty have morphed into wave after successive wave of new Canadians of every hue in God's earth. The Irish street names finding themselves host to African mosques and Indian cafes and Chinese laundries. The alleyways and lanes covered daily in a babble of languages from every hot spot of the Globe. But the same Christmas Eve scenes remain, the causes and faces different, but the same old.

Oh yes, I met Molly again too. I bumped into her on the street and I dearly wish I hadn't. I recognized her right way, she had hardly changed at all. Except her face that is. The impish smile was gone, long gone. I never saw her eyes, she wears sunglasses all the time now because of the light. The rest of her face is frozen into a mask as if she had taken an overdose of that Botox, but I know that other drugs are guilty. She couldn't smile now if she wanted to. But I don't think she wants to anyway. Her breezy, manner and hot temper flattened out by drugs. Her memory full of holes, her speech slurred, her mind wandering. She was buying drugs at the time. I gave her twenty bucks. She wandered off with not a backward glance.

And that is the story of the three wise men from two decades ago. Each having followed our respective stars, I guess you can say. Floyd? Gone, nobody knows where, nobody cares, it seems. He is hardly a memory in a part of town where he was once a prince of the streets. Mickey? Still in prison for all I know. Either that or dead or broken somewhere. Me? A Salvation Army officer in Regent Park.

That Christmas Eve...did it mean anything? Was it a window of grace that God cracked open to give Floyd and Mickey a chance to follow a different star, take a different path in life? A long shot at the straight and narrow for them? A Christmas gift orchestrated by God for a couple of his blacker, black sheep?

Or was it not really about Floyd and Mickey at all, but just about getting those one hundred toys to those one hundred children that night? God often uses strange midwives to birth his goodness in our fallen world... Pharoah, Rahab, to name a couple. But if so, why those kids in that place in that particular year? What was special about them?

Or maybe it was primarily about me and my responsibility? Maybe it was chance opened for me. A chance to talk to Floyd and Mickey, to influence them, to save them. A chance I obviously blew.

As each Christmas passes and the memory comes alive for me again, though dimming and fading each year, it seems that the need to invest it with some sort of meaning grows more important, urgent even. Christmas should be about hope, not regret, it seems to me.

Maybe it was just a lesson about choices and common grace. Something to mull over as I stand and collect money for The Salvation Army every Christmas, whistling carols to myself.

"The hopes and fears of all the years are met in thee tonight."

Indeed.

Chapter 18: Under the Bridge

I MET LONELINESS ONE NIGHT. THAT'S SOMETHING THAT DOESN'T happen often, not to the majority of people, not to coddled folks like myself who have lived safe and warm and adequately loved since the day of our birth. Granted, most of us have been alone from time to time, often by choice; a few of us may have even flirted with Loneliness, danced a turn or two with her, and moved on. We've never had to stay; the luxury of choice has been our pleasurable right.

But anyway, I met her one night. I walked around a corner and there she stood, large as life, smack in my face. I felt an icy blast of desolation and looking up, saw her—cocky and promiscuous, leaning against the wet, mossy brickwork, her flesh all cold and grey and pierced by shadows; that bitter old Moloch of the lost, the princess Loneliness herself.

I was too startled to be truly afraid. Who wouldn't have been? I'd never seen such a sight.

She had a brazen thrust to her scabrous jaw and deceitful eyes that smoked with a carnivorous patience, as if certain in the knowledge that sooner or later everyone would succumb to her stifling embrace. Many do, I mused, but not all—not me. I belong to Another. She knew it and her drove her crazy. I looked straight into her cold, hard eyes. I looked straight through the rouge, the dye, the cheap perfume of forgotten strangers and spoke to her marrow. I told her the name of my Master.

She careened off the wall in a fit of poisonous rage. She knew that my companions and I were here with purpose; she knew we came wanting. We'd come looking for some lost souls that she had claimed squatter's rights on.

'They're mine!' she screamed, and spilled hot tears of cold hate down her lurid face. 'They belong to me! This is my place, my home, my kingdom! Mine! Mine! Mine!'

'Wrong,' our Presence said (it's a good thing to travel with truth as your bodyguard—life becomes rougher for sure, but sweet victories such as these make up for it). 'Wrong, wrong, wrong,' said our blue-black shadow suits and taut crimson cap bands. 'Wrong,' said our pocket Bibles. 'Wrong', said said the styrofoam cups of hot chocolate. 'Wrong, wrong, wrong,' chuckled the prayers that swirled 'round our heads like clean and shiny wraiths.

We ignored her in the end, brushing past her with finality. Loneliness was a sovereign ignominiously shamed in her own fiefdom. She exploded off into the false night of the city, howling in rage and embarrassment, strewing imprecations and curses in her wake. We knew she'd be back as soon as we left. We walked on.

We knew where the lost ones would be sleeping, and wouldn't have needed the watery beam of the flashlight but for the mud, the holes, the grassy clumps and old railway track that passed for the good earth. Garbage, spilled like popcorn, made walking a studied process. From time to time the moon snagged a smudge of trash and invested it with a dirty glow exalting it with borrowed glory.

We came upon them, their pile of wood, blankets and ancient mattresses. 'Home, Sweet, Home,' someone had scratched into the concrete abutment of the bridge. The scribe must have been sober, for the words were straight and proportionate, and that meant it was not a joke. Someone knew what they were doing, someone had thought about it and deliberately drew such lines, so clear and bold, so full of bitter irony. So we looked away, shamed by our possession of this longed-for reality.

I cleared my throat to herald our arrival. The awkward lunging beneath the tumble of blankets slowly came to a halt. A couple of faces popped out. Realization became recognition. Grimy, copper faces broke into wide, incomplete smiles. The musical tones of their native tongue broke over us like sunlight on a fall day—and we were welcomed. Truly, they were glad to see us. They were honest-to-God happy for the interruption of our presence. That's a beautiful miracle to be sure. How many people, who say every day, 'Glad to see you', really are? Precious few. Such honesty of reaction (and the pendulum swings both ways) is a strange gift that the Good Lord has allowed to flourish among the have-nots. One stumbles upon grace in the strangest places.

And we were glad to see them. Hadn't we searched for them, driven halfway across the bowels of the city and walked through mud and reek to share their company under this bridge? Didn't we do it every week? To bring some food (more sacrament than sustenance) and some affordable conversation, to pray with them and for them, to show them that we care? We were walking proof that the Good Lord hadn't totally forgotten them. We explained it rather well.

Why though? Merely to salve our consciences rubbed raw through evangelical exhortation? Just to get that rush of do-good-feel-good adrenaline? Is that it? Is that why? Were we merely soul-scalp hunters offering hot chocolate and blankets in exchange for a verbal confession of salvation, cheaply earned? Gospel hustlers cashing in on a bargain basement opportunity?

Why? Why? Some nights I know, other nights I'm not so sure. Another thing I've learned, another little rule I've picked up along the way, is that one shouldn't examine too hard. Believers who spend a disproportionate amount of time navel-gazing can get a crick in the neck from looking inward too long. Have I ever performed any act of charity, any deed of love, from completely pure, snow-white motives, swept clean of any selfishness, any consideration of gain or profit, any goad of guilt? I don't think so. Have you?

I've long since learned the futility of trying to monitor my motives. At the bottom of it all is that I do it for God (as broad a statement as one is ever likely to make) and from that all the rest gets piled on. I doubt, in my fallen state, if I could ever do anything clothed in purity of intent from start to finish. That would mean that everything leading up to that act, at that moment, would have to be utterly devoid of my humanness—every fleeting thought and lust, every self-centred hesitation. It would mean that every consequent ripple that emanated from that act henceforth would have to remain equally untainted. Impossible. Unless, that is, I was perfect. Totally holy, every word, every thought, with every action as pure as the sparkling water of a mountain stream.

I would have to be God. And I'm not—not by a long shot. Like most people, my life has been one long struggle between those twin duelists, carnality and holiness. One long mixed motive, with a bias toward the truth, I'm hoping.

One thing I do know. Linda and Darrell and Leo and OkeeDokee aren't much concerned by all this. They enjoy the chocolate and appreciate the sandwiches. They weep their sorrows into our clean ears and wipe their snotty noses on the hard edges of our crisp epaulets. They let us pray with them (do they hear?) and even, on occasion, tell us a joke (never funny and usually dirty).

The mystery of our motives is best left on the discussion table. The Good Lord has promised to weigh and sift through everything we do in His name come Judgement Day anyway. Why should I worry about it? I do my best and leave the reasoning up to Him. I'll take my chances.

I mean, we chased that old harlot Loneliness away, didn't we? Even if only for a few minutes. But when you're down and out and lost and long since past any redemptive yearnings that society might've once had for you, a few minutes can seem like an eternity. That's got to count for something.

Chapter 19:
Nomads, Gypsies and Secret Agents

"Man is an animal suspended in webs of significance that he himself has spun. I take culture to be those webs ... and the analysis of it to be therefore not an experimental science in search of law but an interpretive one in search of meaning."—Clifford Geertz

"Own only what you can always carry with you: know languages, know countries, know people. Let your memory be your travel bag."—Alexander Solzhenitsyn

"In Ljublana, the capital of Slovenia, I once met an 87-year-old man. He told me that he had lived his entire life in the same place, yet at the same time he had lived in seven different countries."
—Javier Solana, Secretary General of NATO

THE PROBLEM WITH 'CONVENTIONAL WISDOM' IS THAT IT is usually more parts convention than wisdom. As evangelicals, we are particularly given to accepting conventional wisdom. An idea is birthed, a fresh term coined, a new paradigm offered up on the bookstands and the speaking circuit and we, in our ceaseless quest for formulas, accept it as truth, rarely challenging or subjecting it to critical assessment.

One negative result is that we often can become captives of definitions that we ourselves have put in place and rarely consider the need to step outside the boundaries of those categories we believe to be true and fixed. We become prisoners of paradigms created by ourselves or given by others.

The evangelical paradigm of 'cross-cultural missions' is a term (and an understanding) that essentially defines cross-cultural as the crossing of one, at the most two, boundaries. Those of culture and/or language. Certainly these are valid boundaries but I think that they are not as definitive as we have come to believe and there are others that are rarely, if ever, considered. We allow these to remain intact in our lives as untouched and uncrossed as distant frontier posts.

I believe the normal Christian life to be one of constant and continuous cross-cultural tension in which the Christian, the serious, mission-minded believer, is seeking not only to cross boundaries wherever he may find them, but also does his utmost to reject all boundaries, attempting to live the majority of his life outside of his 'culture', like a soldier behind enemy lines.

I would broaden the definition of cross-cultural to an all-encompassing worldview that assumes a centrality in our thinking of mission, rather than one periphery aspect of mission as it is generally now defined. In this understanding virtually every encounter, every day, becomes an opportunity for 'cross-cultural' engagement and becomes a choice for the missionary to either stay within, or to step out of, preconfigured boundaries.

The normal (ideal) Christian life is one of pilgrimage, of life lived with a light hold on the world and its treasures and values. We are to live in a holy tension with all that surrounds us, never leaving yet never cleaving (John 17:15-18). Eternal strangers, yet everywhere at home, citizens of a different reality with only the Lord and his

Kingdom claiming our ultimate allegiance and loyalty. Like spies we should be able to move easily and smoothly in and out of the cultural pools, provincial prejudices and comfort zones erected by the nations and the tribes, including our own.

Indeed, the hymnology of my denomination is rife with such understanding. Historical precedent abounds. 'Every land is my Fatherland—because every land in my Father's', claimed one of our Generals. The following memo was sent out in the summer of 1882 to English Salvation Army officers preparing to head to India as missionaries:

"Remember that you are likely to be absolutely alone—it may be for months together...in the villages the men must expect to have no furniture at all, except some mats, and must learn to sit on the ground like a tailor...you will have to learn to cook just as Indians do and to wash your clothes at the stream with them...You must make up your mind to leave entirely forever and behind you all your English ideas and habits..." (*The General Next to God*, Richard Collier)

The parting advice given to the leader of these intrepids, a man by the name of Tucker was: 'Get into their skins, Tucker!' And so he did.

"It came home to Tucker that the... greatest problem was the rigid stratification of caste—and the souls he sought were those of India's sixty million outcastes."

"Tucker now took an epoch-making decision: to win these people, his soldiers, now reinforced from England, must embrace the life the outcastes lived. He pared his party's subsistence allowance down to 3s. 6d. a week. English boots were out-of-place; from now on they went barefoot, like mendicant friars. Only later, after some had contracted sunstroke through the soles of the feet, did Tucker relent and allow weaker spirits to don sandals. Their clothing was the Indian fakir's saffron robes of renunciation.

"Along with English clothing, they sloughed off English names. William Stevens, a former jeweller from Worthing, Sussex, who paid for his training by melting and selling the gold in shop aptly became Yesu Ratnam (Jewel of Jesus). Clara Case, a wealthy farmer's daughter, was now Nurani (Shining Light); Tucker himself was Fakir Singh, the Lion of God. Others took names translating as Messenger of Truth and Lion of Comfort."

"For Tucker's force, soon to total 479 officers, no sacrifice was too great if it meant winning souls. To reach the Tamils of Southern India, the men shaved their heads Tamil-fashion, leaving only a round patch of hair coiled in a queue, at the crown and back of the head. Their foreheads bore a patented Salvation Army castemark—red, yellow and blue. To win the Bheels, a stocky diminutive warrior tribe in the jungles of Bombay Presidency, Ensign Carl Winge, the Swede assigned to them, adopted the tribal bow and arrow and brass earrings. For women officers the brass anklets of Bheel wives became regulation. And the Bheels, who had no elaborate religion like the Hindus, proved worth the winning: four hundred of them enrolled under Booth's banner. In time Winge brought them to love God as an embodiment of perfection, to look on prayer as a communion with all that was ultimate, beautiful and everlasting."

"Tucker's troops took pride in Indianisation. They cleaned their teeth with charcoal, like all peasants did, washing from a brass bowl; their simple meals of curry and water were eaten cross-legged on the floor. They came to budget like misers: language lessons were given in the sand to avoid wasting paper. "Hallelujah!" one new arrival exulted in a letter home, "I haven't been in a bed since coming here but sleep on the ground... my feet are swollen and ulcerated with the first week's work and visiting... but to see the happy faces of the converts makes up for everything."

"So warmly did they welcome this nomad hardness that one group of officers, offered money, refused it point-blank. They still had a spare rupee whose use defeated them until they decided to save it for stamps."

Apparently to my forebears, any border was transient, any frontier crossable, any boundary breakable. We have become cautious with age, however. The radicality of The Salvation Army's understanding of 'cross-cultural' was explosively revolutionary in the culture of Victorian England and the British Empire. Booth-Tucker and his team met opposition not so much from the Indians as from the British ruling establishment.

But surely these were fanatics, expressing an impossible ideal. Something not applicable for most of us. We pledge allegiance to certain flags and will not let go, each time undermining in various degrees our ability to be truly cross-cultural. If our first allegiance is to the Kingdom of God and all other allegiances—ranging from that of the nuclear family unit to that our national orientation—are to be subject to this, this means that for the sake of the lost, we 'unhinder' ourselves of all that would slow us down, blunt our edge, dull our senses and render us ineffective.

In the book *Community in Mission*, Phil Needham highlights this vital, yet oft-neglected side, of the Christian identity: "Pilgrims are literally people who journey, often in foreign lands. The image of the Church as a band of pilgrims embodies three key aspects of the Church's life in the world. First, it defines the Church as a people on the move. Second, it articulates the tentativeness of the Church's relationship to the social structures and behavioural patterns of contemporary society. And third, it suggests a Church which is moving towards the future..." (Chapter Three, Called to a Journey: *The Pilgrim People*)

Are we tentative in our relationships to social structures and behavioural patterns of society and culture? Are we 'unhindered' for mission? It is not something to comes to us naturally, but like an spiritual discipline, needs to be worked at, practiced and crafted. If we are committed to mission then we will learn to 'unhinder'.

* * *

I want to identify three boundaries that can hinder us and that need to be considered and dealt with for the sake of effective mission.

1) PATRIOTISM (CULTURE). Patriotism is the acceptable face of nationalism and yet, the concept of patriotism, ('patriot: a person who vigorously supports his country and its way of life', *Collins Concise Dictionary*) finds little Scriptural justification. Of course it is not a bad thing in most cases—for the average person. But for the missionary it is one of the main hindrances to living truly 'cross-culturally'.

Once any culture, country, language group, form of government becomes the standard by which we evaluate and judge others, that is when we start to lose Kingdom perspective. Allegiance to Christ and citizenship in the Kingdom of God should be the only point of reference for such evaluations (Colossians 3:11). The mission the only defining factor. The more we become 'culture-bound' and hindered with patriotism, the less easily we can move amongst the 'tribes and nations'.

'As we become more self-centred and more individualistic we enter into other cultures with greater difficulty... what is called for from us is a self-denials that is completely against the grain of our culture.' (Paul Dekar)

How many of would willingly heed the instructions of that memo of 1882 regarding the mission strategy for India: 'You must make up your mind to leave entirely forever behind you all your English ideas and habits...' ?

2) MATERIALISM. The fact is that most of us in the West simply do not want to give up our toys. We develop a theology wherein *wants* subtly become *needs*; luxuries become ministry tools and comforts are in reality God's blessings and thereby de facto approval of our mission. Thus hindered, we stagger across boundaries, barely able to lift our legs over the barriers, overweight and dressed all wrong. Rather than jettisoning such trinkets prior to mission, we justify retaining such by attempting to bring these dubious blessings to the people to who we wish to engage in mission. Whether they need them, whether they want them, whether they will 'help or hinder', we do not ask. We will not give them up so we accommodate our strategy to include them.

3) RELIGION (TRADITIONALISM). More often than we are probably aware, and more often than we like to admit, it is our religion that creates one of the biggest barriers to mission and to crossing boundaries. The prophets were killed over religion. All of Jesus' disputes with the Pharisees and Sadducees were over religious picayune. Take any bad example from the history of the church starting with the Crusades or the Spanish Inquisition right to your own home church and the wearisome bickering over music styles. The problem is the same—religion as traditionalism.

Cross-culturally it seems to be the rule to mix our religion (our 'extra-biblical codexes of salvation' as someone aptly termed it) and our faith and offer the rather confusing result as the truth, the gospel—we confuse people. And we are willing to fight for our religion and defend it biblically if necessary. Booth was willing to tinker with his religion to get at the sinners. We have allowed our rich traditions to fossilize into traditionalism, and mission effectiveness is always the first to suffer in such circumstances.

This is a big issue and I would suggest anyone missionary who wants to get a handle on it to read *Christianity Rediscovered* by Vincent J. Donovan (see reading list). Can we deconstruct our religion and forgo our traditions enough to allow the Gospel message to blaze brightly and in power?

* * *

So what is to be done? We need to deconstruct the 'cross-cultural' paradigm and realize that the minute one seriously commits to be becoming a follower of Christ and decides to engage in mission, one also makes a decision to become a cultural orphan. We are adopted by God as his children but we abandon our 'parent' culture. This is more of a process than a crisis and only as we mature and are able to keep our mission focus true and firm do we develop the ability to identify and discern barriers to mission that we need to remove. We must resist the urge to settle down and stake a claim in a particular place or people. This is very hard and everything within us fights against it—few of us are naturally pilgrims, we all long for a home, for a sense of security and the familiar. It is something learned, something fought and sacrificed for. The cost is tremendous.

Picture if you can, a man bound by hundreds of barely visibly strings, wrapped tightly around his body, pinning his arms to his sides and his feet together. Many of these he does not he notice and many he sees but does not recognize. As each of these strings is broken, greater freedom of movement is allowed—the maximum freedom and mobility occurs when all the strings have been broken.

Thus it is with the confines of culture that we inherit and assume as part of the trappings of growing up where we grew up and with whom we grew up. Many we willing wrap around ourselves, (materialism) many we are taught are good and even possibly necessary (patriotism), some we are instructed in even by the church (religion, tradition), some result from societal sins (racism, sexism).

Behavioural norms, cultural mores, respectability, acceptability—barriers exist in various forms both inside the community of believers and outside in the world at large. Sociologists claim that such define and hold together society and in many ways they do. Ultimately, however, they stem from sin and are evidence of the separation and alienation of man from God and subsequently man from man. As such, they need to be viewed from a Kingdom perspective that acknowledges them as realities but treats them as more hindrance than help with regard to mission.

As always, true freedom is much too terrifying a concept for most people and for any institution so we buy into existing boundaries and even create our own. The alternative is to throw off the traces and step out into uncharted territory, it is to risk and maybe lose. Forsaking country and culture, comforts and our religious identities if necessary, to run unhindered with the Spirit. No safety net, no guarantees but that God is smiling on us and that, for most of us, is a bad bargain.

So we set the boundaries of what we are willing to do, where we are willing to go and how far. We predestine our mission effective-ness and live content within such limitations. But what if they are false—paper tigers of our own creation? Or worse—one of the devil's ruses, in order to render us ineffectual in the war, in order to hinder us?

How far are you willing to go for the sake of the mission, for the sake of the lost?

'Though I am free and belong to no man, I make myself a slave to everyone, to win as many as possible. To the Jews I became like a Jew, to win the Jews. To those under the law I became like one under the law (though I myself am not under the law), so as to win those under the law. To those not having the law I became like one not hav-ing the law (though I am not free from God's law but under Christ's law), so as to win those not having the law. To the weak I became weak, to win the weak. I have became all things to all men so that by all possible means I might save some.' (1 Corinthians 9:19-23)

This is Paul at his most radical, though I fear that familiarity with the text has dulled the edge for most of us. This is the definitive statement in 'cross-cultural' mission. This is Paul the pragmatist, the realist—hot-tempered and impatient—yet a brilliant tactician, as he rages against the petty confines of safe faith and measured, risk-free mission. This is Paul saying that he will venture into bandit-infested hinterlands, brave raging seas, suffer the wrath of religious fanatics, the might of the Roman Empire, the prejudice of the Greek intellectual community. He will go anywhere, do anything, be anyone and lose his life if necessary (and it was) to cross any barrier—geographical, cultural, social, religious for the sake of the mission, for the sake of the lost.

So what is the call? For stateless, rootless, internationalists, owing no particular allegiance to any one country or culture? Willing to give up all, from family to material comforts to life itself for the cause? For God-fearing nomads, gypsy missionaries, spies and secret agents who can cross frontiers in the dark of night, change identities at the drop of a hat, sleep in a palace and a pig-sty and converse with both king and commoner? Is that what we are talking about?

Is it achievable? Is it desirable? Is it necessary?

It is the gospel, I am afraid. The doctrine of the incarnation is God's cornerstone for the whole salvation story and on this hinged the redemption of the nations in Jesus. It hinges on this today as we, following the example laid down for us by Christ, seek to incarnate this same gospel that recognizes neither 'Greek or Jew, circumcised or uncircumcised, barbarian, Scythian, slave or free, male nor female' (Colossians 3:11 and Galatians 3:26). As we embody this message, as we incarnate it in our world it is only to the degree that we are successful in doing so that the kingdom will come.

* * *

'Of the 360 million people in the European Union alone, nearly a quarter are between 15 and 29 years old. Despite popular notions of "union", they have little sense of shared identity. They are living within the context of no context. The fragmented politics—of gender, race, religion and sexual preference—that characterize the waning years of the 20th century serve only to splinter the youth further...' (The New Youth by Elizabeth Gleick, Time, 1998)

'La generation salle d'attente'—the waiting room generation. Waiting for what? Waiting for whom? In the midst of such a splintering of identities and loyalties, in a world literally torn apart by nationalism and religio-ethnic conflicts and where it seems that the horrors of the twentieth-century are but a practice run for what awaits us in the millennium—what brings reconciliation? In a world where the map is not only being redrawn but quickly discarded as countries as entities lose their prominence and the coming generation will more naturally turn on MTV than stand for their national anthem—who will have credibility?

The what remains the same—the gospel good news.

The who is the question.

'When we have really understood the actual plight of our contemporaries, when we have heard there cry of anguish and when we have understood why they won't have anything to do with our disembodied Gospel, when we have shared their sufferings, both physical and spiritual, in their despair and their desolation, when we have become one with the people of all nations and of the universal church, as Moses and Jeremiah were one with their own people, as Jesus identified himself with the wandering crowds, "sheep without a shepherd," then we will be able to proclaim the word of God—but not until then!' (Jacques Ellul)

SUGGESTED READING LIST:

Wild Hope, Tom Sine.

Monarch Publications Limited, 1991.

A wake-up call to the challenges and opportunities of the 21st Century. Dr. Sine is a Christian and a consultant in futures research for both Christian and secular organizations

Rediscovering Christianity, Vincent J. Donovan.

Orbis Books, 1978.

Father Donovan is a Roman Catholic priest who wrote this book after 17 years of mission work in Tanzania. A fascinating account of the true meaning of missionary work and what the gospel truly is when stripped of its cultural accretions from the West.

Seven Pillars of Wisdom, T.E. Lawrence.

Penguin Books, 1926.

T.E. Lawrence (better known as Lawrence of Arabia) was not a Christian. Yet this classic military chronicle of the desert war in Arabia during WWI serves as one of the best explorations of cross-cultural adaptation ever written.

Captain Richard Francis Burton, Edward Rice.

HarperCollins, 1991.

One of the most fascinating figures of Victorian England, Burton was not a Christian and lived a life in many ways contrary to the Gospel. His ability to live cross-culturally was legendary however, and sets a standard that has likely never been matched, in or out of the church.

Chapter 20: Declaring an Amnesty

"The mass of men lead lives of quiet desperation"—Thoreau

"...you should act and speak as men who will be judged by the law of freedom. The man who makes no allowances for others will find none made for him. It is still true 'that mercy smiles in the face of judgement.' "—James 2: 13, *J.B. Phillips*

"But if you do not forgive men their sins, your Father will not forgive your sins."—Matthew 6:15, *NIV*

"In Latin, to bless is benedicere, which means literally: saying good things. The Father wants to say, more with his touch than with his voice, good things of his children. He has no desire to punish them. They have already been punished excessively by their own inner or outer waywardness. The Father wants simply to let them know that the love they have searched for in such distorted ways has been, is, and always will be there for them. The Father wants to say, more with his hands than with his mouth: "You are my Beloved, on you my favor rests."—Henri J.M. Nouwen, *The Return of the Prodigal Son*

THE ROMAN CATHOLICS INVADED TORONTO IN THE SUMMER of 2002 for World Youth Day and gave a lesson to many of us on the nature of faith and witness. It was the most

Christian event to have taken place in the country in ages. The name of Jesus and the message of the cross were nightly news on the TV and quoted on the front page of all the national newspapers—it was brilliant. One thing the Catholics did was to erect several hundred confessional booths in a park in the city's West end in order to hear the confessions of the pilgrims. "Confession, the sacrament of penance, is a gift, a moment of peace. They can pour their hearts out and be reminded of the goodness within them. So many ...people have a poor self-image", explained one priest. Confession in the Catholic church is now termed the "sacrament of reconciliation". To some of my more conservative evangelical friends it was dismissed as the only (inadequate) thing the Catholics could offer their people—a way station on their endless cycle of sin. To me it suggested a profounder understanding of grace than maybe we evangelicals are willing—or able—to grasp.

* * *

I think that there are dozens, hundreds, maybe thousands of pastors throughout Canada and the United States who live their daily lives and work their ministries in various stages of "quiet desperation", due to the fact that somewhere along the line they messed up and sinned. Maybe it was an isolated incident, maybe more than once—a pattern emerging... Whatever the cause and effect, they gave in and are now trapped. Like one of those bottles that we hang up in the summer months to catch wasps and flies, once the victim crawls in there is no way back. That's how it is if you are in ministry in the church, if you are a leader in evangelical circles. Who do you tell? How do you tell? There is no one to talk to and nowhere to go. The price to be paid is too high. The higher up the ladder you may have climbed, the farther the fall and so the deeper you bury it and more trapped you become.

Admitting falliability may be hard simply due to pride. But even pride aside, the reality is that there simply is no way to admit that you have failed. Failure in our driven, corporate and success inspired culture is the unforgiveable sin. Truth has a way of outing itself though and so the fear becomes a daily, aching burden, a flickering fear awaiting the day all will be "proclaimed from the roofs."

The fact is we all mess up, we all sin...every single one of us. If you are reading this and you're alone sitting in a room or an office—raise your hand if you've messed up, if you have crossed some sort of a line somewhere, at some time, and even though you didn't linger there for very long and may have quickly hopped back over, you still crossed that line and you carry that with you night and day... Sound familiar? But what to do with it, how to shake it off, put it behind, get on with life and calling and faith?

Following Nathan's confrontation, David admitted that he had sinned (and rather more terribly and thoroughly than most of us will ever sin). But in his repentance Psalm, he points out to God that: "Against you and you only have I sinned..." Sin, once committed, is largely a matter between the sinner and their God. Other people are usually involved and this hurt and damage needs to be addressed. The main issue, however, is between God and prodigal. So although we may sin against God first off, repentance to God alone is not really an option.

I guess one thing that appeals to me about the Catholics is that, everything else aside, they would take my humanity seriously, if I gave them the chance. Evidence of a weak and compromised theology, my Jobian friends would say. Maybe... Then again, maybe they are just more realistic than we evangelicals, more practical. Maybe the Catholics know the world and understand the human heart better than us because they've been around longer. They know that people are frail and give into temptation and are prone to sin. This is our human side. This is our legacy of living as fallen creatures in a fallen world.

The Catholic concept of calling, of the priesthood, differs from most evangelical concepts of ministry calling. They have more of a "once-a-priest-always-a-priest-and-besides-its-a-thing-between-you-and-God" sort of theology. We would have a hard time getting our heads around how they view their leaders (priests) but at least they have some clarity about the nature of the call and the life of service. It is a developed and sure theology. It is a clarity woefully lacking in most evangelical circles, my own denomination in particular. Maybe because of this, the Catholics own their prodigals far more readily than we Protestants, we evangelicals. They send them to retreat houses and try to heal and restore them in most cases. Their bent is to deal in mercy, dispense grace and maintain respect for their fallen colleagues. The Catholic church defrocks with far more reluctance and fear than we do in giving the boot to an errant leader. Our eagerness for condemnation and swift judgement is a little embarrassing.

The recent sex scandals involving priests in the United States has garnered an enormous amount of media attention. It is a henious thing these priests have done. No one, the Catholic church included, is disputing this but quietly in the background grace is moving. At a conference of Major Superiors of Men, an association of Catholic Orders (about half of all American priests belong to these orders) last year, a decision was made, after a vote, not to cut the errant priests loose, but to work to restore them. The order felt strongly that their approach should be guided by the Catholic belief of redemption for sinners. "Just as a family does not abandon a member convicted of serious crimes, we cannot turn our backs on our brothers", a spokesman said. I wonder how most evangelical denominations would have handled this?

Dr. Tony Campolo was asked by President Clinton to be one of his three spiritual advisors after the Monica Lewinsky scandal broke. This request and Tony's subsequent acceptance of the offer brought a firestorm down on his head. He was pilloried by the evangelical community, accused of all manner of motives and judged with a certainty and swiftness that would have made the Pharisees of Jesus' day green with envy. And remember, Tony was only in the position of counselling a sinner. He had not sinned himself, although he might as well have. I remember how Tony broke down at a conference we were both speaking at in Los Angeles during this time, as he shared about the viciousness of the attacks on him. One pastor wrote: "Don't you understand that this man does not deserve grace?"

Evangelicals have high standards, maybe impossibly high. We are prone to an unconscious dualism, all but ignoring our humanity to instead invest almost solely in idealizing and striving for divinity. When a leader's humanity rears up, when the "old man" refuses to stay dead, it is an affront to our convictions and so the instinctive reaction is to distance the church or organization from the sinner in order to preserve intact our reputations and integrity. The one will be sacrificed for the sake of the many. He or she will be cut loose and isolated. Kind of like the Amish practice of "shunning".

For many of us, our heritage in the Holiness movement is an

added pressure. Our second blessing paradigm has oftimes edged out our tolerance for mercy and grace. Doubtful of the possibility of resurrection once we've blown it, we crucify with almost undecent haste. Indeed, we shoot our wounded.

While serving as a missionary in Russia I learned that while nowhere in the theology of the Orthodox Church was there instruction or teaching to worship icons, I came to understand that the reality "on the street" was different. Most of the little old ladies who haunted the churches daily in droves to light candles and pray, for all intents and purposes did worship the icons. They bowed down to them, kissed them, prayed to them and bought replicas of them to carry around with them. Whatever the Church Fathers may have taught, the foot soldiers lived a different reality.

It is often much the same with us. Whatever John Wesley did believe about perfectionism (hard to get a straight answer on this and if you think you've got it nailed, try reading his journals sometime) and whether or not the holiness proponents in my own tradition were, at the end of the day, prophetic theologians or simply devout men who built theologies around personal experience—the understanding is that we live under the threat of an all but unobtainable goal. I was weaned on this as an evangelical, as a preacher's kid. It is an all-pervasive understanding, an embedded conventional wisdom that sets us all up for failure.

Leaders are expected to be perfect. To sin is to admit weakness and failure and to invite punishment. Such is the church culture that we are a part of. Why is it that the most common reaction to the word holiness seems to be fear? If you think about it, it is an odd and even profane reaction. Fear as an instinctive, gut reaction to the winsome, attractive character of Jesus, the most holy of people. Why is this? Because we have little experienced this face of holiness, we have experienced something else in its place, something that smacks of legalism and fear. I sometimes wonder if we are among the most graceless of God's people. The word in the trenches is this: If you mess up, keep it hidden or you'll get crucified. Jesus claimed that his Father desired mercy, not sacrifice, but we know different—it is sacrifice and not mercy that will be extracted.

And we evangelicals pick our sins, do we not? Illicit sex, financial impropriety, addictions, abortion, divorce, homosexuality—all the obvious biggies. Yet simultaneously will accommodate such things as materialism and consumerism, worldliness, power and control issues, theological infidelity and hate, to name a few. If God has a hierarchy of sins these latter are surely the worst. It is sins like these that can displace God in our hearts, raise up true idols and slowly rot the fabric of our souls. The others? Bad enough, to be sure. But things that someone can move beyond, can get over, can pick themselves up from and dust themselves off and keep walking. If there is a helping hand to grip and not a heavy hand that spanks and pushes down and away.

So here is my idea. It is a gamble almost as risky as the one God took that dark afternoon on Calvary. Hold a denominational jubilee year. Announce an amnesty! I'm issuing a challenge, I suppose. If our denominational and ministry heads are chosen and hired by us but also appointed by God, then the challenge is for them to be the "Father" in the parable of the prodigal son. Could a denominationl head not travel from one end of his or her area of responsibility, stopping in strategically targeted towns and cities, central points that are announced well beforehand, and in each stop set up shop in a particular place... and wait. Pastors and other leaders within traveling distance would know that on certain days, their leader will be waiting at this certain place... waiting to hear confession. Just like those priests in the park in Toronto, they will dispense the sacrament of reconciliation and pronounce their benedicere. No human resources people present, no lawyers, no pastoral care specialists, no counselors—just the man or woman that God appointed as their spiritual head. Leaders would come to privately confess their sins, receive prayer and absolution and then go on their way. Sins forgiven and forgotten. No retribution, no comebacks, to "... go, and sin no more", as Jesus would say.

I can hear the protests now. Sure it would be messy—but grace is messy. Sure there are people who would take advantage of it. But that's ultimately between them and God, according to David. There are some parameters that would have to be in place and legal breaches might have to be considered. This is all understood. But the concept is doable—it can be done!

It would generate much public criticism in our evangelical world and from the world outside our churches. Our post-Christian societies understanding of grace is as poor as ours and their bent is to hold us Christians to higher standards than they would ever ask of themselves. But I also believe it would garner much private admiration. I believe it would bring freedom and release back into the church. Good pastors, good leaders, long paralyzed by a bad choice or haunted by a moment of weakness, would be set free to once again move ahead with their calling and ministry. It would bring grace back into our pulpits and pews. Grace which would then flow out onto the streets and into the offices and homes of our countries, reestablishing a trust long broken and dispelling fear. "He has sent me to proclaim freedom for the prisoners... to release the oppressed, to proclaim the year of the Lord's favor", Jesus declared.

So fling open the closet doors and let's haul out those skeletons and bury them forever! Throw off the shackles of guilt! Get on with life! A new day is coming!

* * *

I have fallen, Lord,
Once more.
I can't go on, I'll never succeed.
I am ashamed, I don't dare look at you.
And yet I struggled, Lord, for I knew you were right near me,
     bending over me, watching
But temptation blew like a hurricane,
And instead of looking at you I turned my head away.
I stepped aside
While you stood, silent and sorrowful,
Like the spurned fiance who sees his loved one carried away
     by the enemy.
When the wind died down as suddenly as it had arisen,
When the lightening ceased after proudly streaking the darkness,
All of a sudden I fond myself alone, ashamed, disgusted,
     with sin in my hands.

This sin that I selected the way a customer makes his purchase,
This sin that I have paid for and cannot return, for the
     storekeeper is no longer there,
This tasteless sin,
This odorless sin,
This sin that sickens me,

That I have wanted but want no more,
That I have imagined,
    sought,
    played with,
    fondled for a long time;
That I have finally embraced while turning coldly away from you,
My arms outstretched, my eyes and heart irresistibly drawn;
This sin that I have grasped and consumed with gluttony,
It's mine now, but it possesses me as the spider-web holds captive
    the gnat.
It is mine,
It sticks to me,
It flows in my veins,
It fills my heart.
It has slipped in everywhere, as darkness slips into the forest at
    dusk and fills all the patches of light.

I can't get rid of it.
I run away from it the way ones tries to lose a stray dog, but it
    catches up with me and bounds joyfully against my legs.
Everyone must notice it.
I'm so ashamed that I feel like crawling to avoid being seen,
I'm ashamed of being seen by my friends,
I'm ashamed of being seen by you, Lord,
For you loved me, and I forgot you.
I forgot you because I was thinking of myself
And one can't think of several persons at once.
One must choose, and I chose.

And your voice
And your look
And your love hurt me.
They weigh me down
They weigh me down more than my sin.

Lord, don't look at me like that,
For I am naked,
I am dirty,
I am down,
Shattered,
With no strength left.
I dare make no promises,
I can only lie bowed before you.

Come, son, look up.
Isn't it mainly your vanity that is wounded?
If you loved me, you would grieve, but you would trust.
Do you think that there's a limit to God's love?
Do you think that for a moment I stopped loving you?
But you still rely on yourself, son. You must rely only on me.

Ask my pardon
And get up quickly.
You see, its not falling that is the worst,
But staying on the ground.

Michel Quoist, *Prayers*

Chapter 21: Thoughts on Hell

"All folks who pretend to religion and grace,
Allow there's a Hell, but dispute of the place;"
—Jonathan Swift

"Excuse me for not answering. I have friends in both places."
—Jean Cocteau, politely declining to offer any opinion when the
   subject of Heaven and Hell was broached in a conversation

"Yes, because it is the dogma of the church—but I don't believe
anyone is in it."
—Abbe Arthur Mugnier, upon being asked if he believed in Hell

I KNOW AT LEAST ONE PERSON IN TOWN WHO IS TERRIFIED OF going to hell. He came out with it once when I was visiting him in prison and took me a little by surprise. He is a tough guy—a little crazy even, some might say. There is not much finesse to him, but a reputation for unpredictability and a lengthy criminal record packed with violence.

On this visit he was awaiting trial, the charges more serious than the crime because he was under surveillance for organized crime activities at the time. He worked for the mob as a low-level enforcer. There didn't seem to be much he was afraid of. The way the other prisoners reacted to him, this certainly seemed to be the case.

He was afraid of Hell, though. After talking for about half an hour about things he had done, a confessional of sorts, he leaned across the table in the visiting room, dropped his voice down low, glanced around the empty visiting room as if there were someone else besides just the two of us and hissed with a low urgency... "I don't want to burn in Hell!".

As I mentioned, this took me by surprise, coming so unexpectedly at the end of a confession session with hardly a warning in sight. It seemed at first that he just blurted it out but then I understood that he had been heading in this direction all along, leading up to it in fact. It was this vivid fear that had been preying on his mind as he sat in prison. Sunday school memories stirred up by the chapel services he had been attending in order to kill time as he waited for his day in court. He was afraid and looking for an out.

Frankly, I did not know what to say not having thought much about Hell lately. I was certainly not used to employing it as an evangelistic method or a ruse to winkle my way into someone's soul in order to get a profession of faith. Lets say it isn't a window of opportunity I am accustomed to climbing through. But then it was not me who brought Hell up.

* * *

We do not talk about Hell much, not in my denomination, not in evangelical circles and definitely not in Canada. Hell remains the domain of the wild-eyed, revivalists who inhabit the barely respectable fringes of evangelicalism; the crazies south of the border in their bad suits and worse accents (yet somehow scads of money to pay for TV time).

Most of us are several generations removed from such crudity and view their antics with distaste. We are more educated, more urbane, more dignified and frankly much more humane than to be scaring people with tales of everlasting torment and unquenchable flames and devils with pitchforks. We know that fear is only good as a short-term motivator, that it wears off pretty quickly. We are surgeons, scalping in with razor-sharp precision on seeker-sensitive terms, not theological thugs bludgeoning our way into people's souls with the doctrine of Hell as our cudgel. Shudder!

I personally cannot remember hearing one single sermon on Hell in, say, the last ten years (not that I'm complaining, mind you). Jonathan Edwards may have been able to convict ranks of New Englanders with his "Sinners in the Hands of An Angry God", but what was effective in 1741 might not play so well in 2004. Besides, I have my doubts about the efficacy of any step of faith motivated primarily by self-preservation.

As is usually the case, there seems to be two hard poles between which the majority of us flounder and flop and eventually position ourselves. On the more liberal (ergo compassionate) side are those who cannot conceive of themselves treating their children or any of their friends in this manner—namely consigning them to a Hell—so naturally enough they transfer this parental indulgence to God. Hell is strange that way. It's the one doctrine that makes otherwise theologically conservative people go soft and wobble into a vague liberalism. People who would would be quite offended if you referred to them as such, nevertheless slide into a gentle universalism in order to get a handle on Hell. Now going this way raises all sorts of questions about God's deep intolerance for sin, his unassailable holiness, not to mention more than a few passages of the Bible that will need some rather clever explaining away. For me it seems too easy an out—way too easy. Why play the game if everybody wins in the end? Why run the race if it's fixed? Common sense says there is a ying to the yang of God's love.

The other side is more hardcore. It's made up of the black-and-whiters who hold fiercely to a kind of "The-Bible-said-it-I-believe-it-that-settles-it / turn-or-burn / Jesus-or-Hell" kind of theology. All Augustinian rigidity and dire consequences. They don't do much for me either. I've never liked bullies—physical or theological. At the end of the day, the hardcore crew seem to enjoy the prospect of Hell far too much for my liking. There is an almost pathological glee about their adamant views on the matter and their careless willingness to consign whole nations into the lake of fire. This raises all sorts of questions about God's essential nature being love, the tremendous pains he has gone through over several thousand years of human history in order to reconcile mankind to him, his utter inability to sin (isn't torture always a sin?), to name a few?

Such people would have had a hard time in Russia. I was constantly fielding queries from first-generation Christians who, as the concept of a Hell dawned on them, wondered if this meant that the past several generations of their countrymen and women, not to mention parents, grand-parents, siblings, friends... were basically—toast? Their lives on earth had been hell enough under Stalin and his cronies—but I'm the guy here to tell them that it was all just a warm-up for the really big one? There was no way on earth! Innate cowardice aside, I didn't really believe it.

I resolved the issue for myself while I was in Russia, about ten years ago, by reading a book entitled "Four Views on Hell". The book consists of four theologians each of whom in turn present their views on Hell, while the other three respond. The four views were: literal, metaphorical, pugatorial and conditional. The denomination I minister in position, according to our 11th doctrine, are literalists. But I must confess that after reading this book, I became a conditionalist, if not a downright annihilationist. Clark Pinnock's rhetoric won the day for me as he eloquently held the line between the demands of a Holy God, the various Biblical hints on some very nasty consequences to sin and the essential quality of God as Love.

The competition consisted of the literalist, John Walvoord of Dallas Theological Seminary, who was predictably unyielding, with the smugness of a convinced inerrantist and the smell of blind faith about him. The metaphoricalist (read as liberal) was William Crockett of Alliance Theological Seminary. He was frankly a little too airy-fairy and high-brow for the average pew warmer to ever comprehend, myself included. Zachary Hayes' defense of purgatory (Catholic Theological Union) was tempting, but too dependent on tradition and not enough on Scripture and overall—a little too weird for a Protestant boy.

But Pinnock hit the nail on the head for me and I became a believer. His convincing theology aside, I figured that any serious Canadian theologian who has consistently resisted the siren-call of the United States, who has had the courage to publicly change his mind and his theology over the years and who chooses to worship and minister in a small, inner-city church—well, he's got my vote.

* * *

As for the guy I visited in prison. He walked. In spite of his past record, in spite of being on probation and in spite of having been caught red-handed, he went free. Amazing what can be done with one of the best lawyers in town on the case. Last I heard he had become a partner in a downtown sports bar, our visiting room chat most probably a distant memory.

But you know what? Theological queries and methodological misgivings aside, I've been thinking lately that I may just walk into that bar one day and remind him of that conversation. A herald of Hell—or a messenger anyway, in a manner of speaking. It seems to be the only chink in his armour and some windows you have to learn to crawl through, even if they just open a crack.